VIRGINIA'S HISTORIC RESTAURANTS

and their recipes

JOHN F. BLAIR, *Publisher*

Winston-Salem, North Carolina

VIRGINIA'S HISTORIC RESTAURANTS

and their recipes

by DAWN O'BRIEN

Drawings by Patsy Faires

Book design by Virginia Ingram
Drawings by Patsy Faires
Cover photograph by Bernard Carpenter
Composition by Graphic Composition, Inc.
Manufactured by Donnelley Printing Company

Library of Congress Cataloging in Publication Data on page 207.

ACKNOWLEDGMENTS Everybody knows that Broadway's financial backers are called angels. But what is the name given to those who back you with a part of themselves, give you the kind of help money can't buy? Are they archangels? I don't know. I do know that they are a special breed of human being, and I am indebted to them for their help.

To: The chefs who gave, taught and encouraged—even the one who spanked my hand when I was reaching for the wrong utensil.

To: The restaurateurs who shared their restaurant's heritage and renovation with me.

To: The artist, Patsy Faires, for her beautiful pen and ink renderings of the restaurants.

To: Marty Rawson, once again my gourmet mainstay, for helping me test, retest and correct many recipes. Also to Saxton Powell, Betty Jo Gilley, Becky Newton, Martha Gay Morton and Bev Wachtel for their testing abilities.

To: My daughter, Daintry, for photographing many of the restaurants, as well as driving, typing and collating material for me many times.

To: John and Julia Bize who encouraged and guided me in the right direction.

To: My husband, John, and daughter, Heather, who chose to encourage rather than complain.

To: All my guinea pigs who ate the testing dishes. They have so quadrupled in number that it's impossible to name all of them.

To: Virginia Ingram, Marcia Harmon and Brenda Johnson who are collectively the most intuitive, creative and kind people with whom I've been privileged to share my work.

To: John Fries Blair for believing in the written word— especially mine, and manifesting his belief so enthusiastically.

FOREWORD

This book is dedicated to my mama, Saxton West Powell, who taught me that life must be lived extravagantly. That doesn't necessarily require material goods or money—it does require panache. My mother said, "Don't just do a job well—any fool can do that. Do it with flair!"

It's taking the mundane and making it exciting, or, at the very least, attractive. In a sense, my mother's philosophy is appropriate for this book because it is precisely what the truly great chefs do. They take raw ingredients and create with a delicious flair.

When I first embarked upon writing this series my daughter, Daintry, said, "The worst that could happen is you might learn how to cook." True, in the beginning I wasn't a great cook. Then, through writing *North Carolina's Historic Restaurants and Their Recipes*, I experienced a kind of on-the-road education, learning from chefs whose training grounds included everything from mama's kitchen to the famed culinary institutes of the world.

Over and over I heard them say that formal schooling is important, but that expertise is achieved through apprenticing with great chefs. That is where the real tricks and secrets are learned. Then, because good cooking is an art form, a chef's individual creativity emerges. This is how their fame is achieved.

By the time I was researching Virginia, my culinary ability was much improved. My younger daughter, Heather, no longer winced at the thought of another "fancy do-dah" meal. While working on the other book, there were times when her dad slipped her money for authentic junk food. But with the testing of the Virginia recipes, I've seen a more appreciative attitude.

As with North Carolina, the impetus for researching Virginia was the same. I have a particular affinity for historic settings and want to see them preserved. Maybe it's because of the values I grew up with, I don't know, but it seems to me that we learn best from history.

I am especially grateful to those who are willing to salvage our past, particularly our historic buildings. A division of the Department of Cultural Resources designates certain over-fifty-year-old structures as historically significant if a note-worthy event has occurred there or if the building displays architectural integrity.

I truly honor all who rescue these historic buildings, but I loudly applaud those who convert them into viable operations—in particular, restaurants. This is because I have found that, for the most part, the renovators/restaurateurs who care enough to salvage the structural remnants of our past put the same intricate care into preparing unusually fine food.

And that is my mama's philosophy—going the extra step to set whatever you do apart from what has been done before.

CONTENTS

Virginia's traditions, our Commonwealth's culture, and our distinct qualities of life since Colonial times are unique. The food given us by the bounty of our land, and the ingenuity Virginians have developed in preparing it are just as unique. The preparation of food in Virginia, and dining in Virginia, are as thoroughly a part of our ethos of cultivated civility as any of the Old Dominion's natural wonders or any of our other customs and habits. To sense and savor the full taste of Virginia, we believe our visitors have to visit both our historic monuments and homes, and dine in our restaurants. In this volume, Dawn O'Brien has developed a fresh, new perspective on a wide variety of typically Virginia restaurants that offer a wide variety of typically Virginian fare.

The variety of restaurants described on the pages that follow, though by no means an exhaustive listing of the eating establishments in which we take such great pride, does capture the essence of the art of preparing food and of dining in Virginia. Beginning with the Tidewater, through which the first Englishmen made their way more than 350 years ago to navigate up the James, Dawn O'Brien traces some of Virginia's outstanding restaurants through the Piedmont region beyond the fall line of the James, and into and over the Blue Ridge mountains, where our heartiest early settlers made immeasurable contributions to our culture and to our way of life in the way they grew, prepared, and consumed the delicacies in food that have become a part of our treasured mountain folklore.

I hope you will enjoy the descriptions in the pages that follow, that you will try the recipes listed in this volume, and that you will come to Virginia to sample and to savor for yourself with knife and fork, the succulent varieties of unique cuisine that, at best, can only be described imperfectly in print.

Charles S. Robb
Governor of Virginia

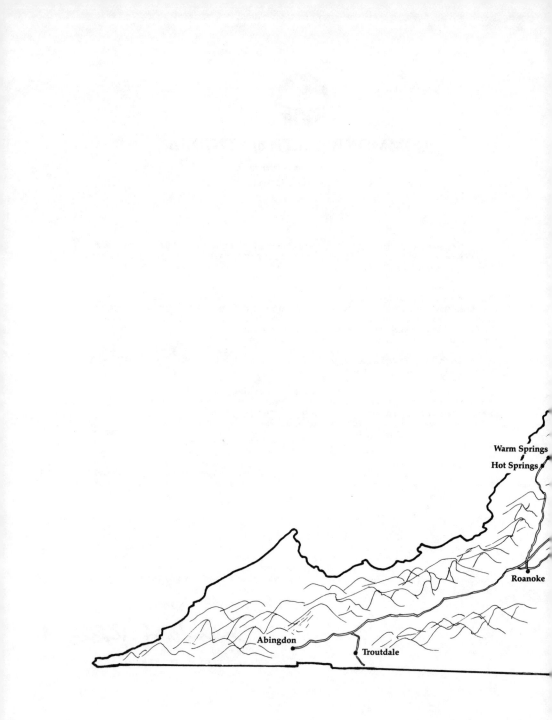

Warm Springs

Hot Springs

Roanoke

Abingdon

Troutdale

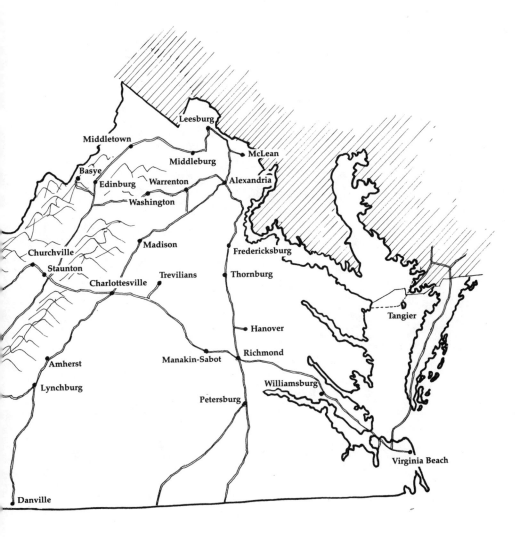

MARTHA WASHINGTON INN
Abingdon

MARTHA WASHINGTON INN

Driving down Main Street in Abingdon, you feel time has become confused. It should be a horse and buggy, not a car, dropping you at the door of the Martha Washington Inn. Today, the inn appears not a stitch different than it did a hundred and fifty years ago when General Francis Preston built this home for his wife and fifteen children.

During subsequent years, the house has served diverse purposes. During the Civil War it was a hospital for both Confederate and Union armies. I was told that sometimes during a full moon the plaintive strains of a violin can be heard. Old-timers insist that the violinist was a young lady who played to ease the pain of her wounded Confederate lover whom she had hidden in the attic when the Yankees took over the hospital.

The inn is a treasure of tales. Stories include the inn's tenure as a girls' school, which was said to have concentrated more on dining room etiquette than academics. And speaking of the dining room, theirs is named the Cameo Room after the girls' yearbook.

Décor and cuisine perform a successful blend of both centuries. The walls are covered in brown velvet with a parade of crystal chandeliers attached as sconces. Among the odd variety of wooden tables are splashes of large green plants.

Having a late dinner in this classic yet comfortable room, my husband, John, and I chose their Coco Shrimp appetizers. These gigantic shrimp are dipped in coconut, then fried. They could easily be a meal in themselves. If you, like my husband, are a beef lover, then the Carpetbagger is their pièce de résistance. John vows that it is the best filet mignon that has ever entered his mouth. My one bite would second that motion, but it was difficult to tear myself away from their equally prized Crab and Shrimp Norfolk.

If you can squeeze it in, dessert is a good old Southern Raisin Bread Pudding or Cherries Jubilee.

A lighter dining choice would be their Fresh Flounder baked

in champagne and herbs. It is accompanied by a house salad and their Dijon Vinaigrette Dressing.

We were pleased to find that the inn's wine list is as simple or lavish as your pocketbook dictates.

It doesn't matter whether you are stopping for breakfast, lunch or dinner, you must not miss seeing the sterling silver banquet table near the lobby. Appraised for $125,000, the table was accidentally stumbled upon in their basement last year.

Steeped in romantic history, we found the inn's food and atmosphere to be the perpetuation of Southern hospitality as it was originally intended.

The Martha Washington Inn is located at 150 West Main Street in Abingdon. Breakfast is served from 7:00 a.m. until 10:00 a.m.; lunch is served from 11:30 a.m. until 2:00 p.m.; and dinner is from 6:00 p.m. until 10:00 p.m., Monday through Saturday. On Sunday, breakfast is served from 7:00 a.m. until noon; brunch is from 9:00 a.m. until 3:00 p.m.; and dinner is from 5:00 p.m. until 9:00 p.m. For reservations (preferred) call (703) 628-3161.

MARTHA WASHINGTON INN'S FLOUNDER FILLET

4 5- to 8-ounce flounder fillets	1 teaspoon pepper
4 12-inch-by 16-inch pieces of brown wrapping paper	2 teaspoons Old Bay Seasoning
1 cup butter, melted	8 lemon slices
1 teaspoon salt	2 carrots, julienned
	2 celery stalks, julienned

Place 4 pieces of paper on counter. Pour ¼ cup melted butter onto each paper's center and spread evenly over paper. Season each paper with ¼ teaspoon salt, ¼ teaspoon pepper, and ½ teaspoon Old Bay Seasoning. Place 2 lemon slices in center of paper and cover with julienned celery and carrot strips. Place fillet upside down on top of carrots and celery. Fold paper together; flatten and crease tightly.

3

Place on greased cookie sheet in 350-degree oven for 7 to 10 minutes. The paper will puff up when done. Take a sharp knife and, cutting an x from corner to corner, peel back. Serves 4.

MARTHA WASHINGTON INN'S
MARTHA'S DELIGHT

4 8-ounce boneless chicken breasts, unskinned
16 ounces country ham, cooked and julienned

rice (follow package directions)

Bake chicken breasts in oven at 350 degrees for about 15 minutes or until done. Heat julienned ham, put over steamed rice, and top with chicken breasts. Cover with Red Eye Gravy (recipe below). Serves 4.

Red Eye Gravy:
fat scraps from country ham
pepper to taste

1 teaspoon cornstarch
3 to 4 drops of coffee

Take all fat and scraps from ham and place in sauté pan and cook down slowly. Take cooked meat scraps from pan and mince finely; return to pan with rendered fat and simmer for approximately 10 to 15 minutes until mixture turns red. Pepper to taste (salt unnecessary). Add about a teaspoon of cornstarch to thicken and a few drops of coffee for color.

THE TROUTDALE DINING ROOM
Troutdale

THE TROUTDALE DINING ROOM

Can you believe fresh rainbow trout caught in the morning by the restaurant's owner?

Fisherman and restaurateur Barry Serber has indeed worn many hats since he and his wife, Carol, both native New Yorkers, came south looking for a new way of life in 1976. Having been in show business in New York, just about the only thing the former comedian knew about restaurants was eating in them. Economists will tell you that the statistics for success with those odds are less than twenty percent. So, why does the Serber's 1906 restaurant become more successful every year? Either the Serbers are fast learners, or they are doing something very special.

Both answers are correct. As Barry said, "You learn fast that standing on a chair that is perched upon a box which is centered on a chest is not the best way to paint a ceiling." That's exactly where Troutdale natives found Barry applying the finishing touches before the old Midway Hotel was converted into a restaurant. Barry and his wife, who is the restaurant's chef extraordinaire, did a lot of refurbishing before their restaurant was launched.

Since the building's exterior appears as if it could be a cousin to the television Walton's place, Carol has decorated the interior to give it the homespun mountain appearance of the early 1900s. My favorite dining room features hand-stenciled blue flowers over whitewashed wood plank walls.

Visual appeal is important, yes, but second only to food. And what they do with food is special. The menu is an ever-changing international delight. I began with Escargot, then sampled my dinner companions' Artichoke with Hollandaise and Liver Pâté Madeira, either one of which I would recommend. Then, knowing the trout was fresh, I ordered it in its decalorized form—poached, Chinese-style. I quickly decided it was just as good as the slivers of Beef Wellington and Veal Piccata I tested, each served with Broccoli and Hollandaise.

For dessert I splurged on the Cheesecake, but snitched

bites of their Mocha Mousse and Flan. The delicate Flan is perfect after a rich meal, but chocolate lovers are going to adore the Mousse. It's all a matter of taste, and the Troutdale Dining Room will have something to titillate the most fussy connoisseur of fine food and drink.

The Troutdale Dining Room is located on Route 16 in Trout-dale. Dinner is served Tuesday through Friday from 5:00 p.m. until 9:30 p.m., and on Saturday and Sunday from 1:00 p.m. until 9:30 p.m., May through October. For reservations call (703) 677-3671.

THE TROUTDALE DINING ROOM'S ESPRESSO ICE CREAM WITH CHOCOLATE KAHLÚA SAUCE

4 egg yolks　　　　　　　**⅓ cup French roast or**
½ cup sugar　　　　　　　　**espresso beans, ground**
3 cups heavy cream

In top of double boiler, beat egg yolks with sugar until dissolved and well blended. In separate pan, scald 2 cups cream with ground beans for 15 minutes. Strain coffee and cream mixture over egg mixture in double boiler. Cook, stirring constantly until the custard coats a spoon. Remove from heat and chill. When chilled, add 1 cup cream, mix well and freeze in ice cream freezer. Mellow a few hours before serving.

Chocolate Kahlúa Sauce:
1 tablespoon sweet butter　　**1 cup cream**
6 ounces semisweet　　　　　**¼ cup Kahlúa or more to**
**　chocolate**　　　　　　　　　**　taste**
¾ cup sugar

In small saucepan melt 1 tablespoon butter. Add chocolate and melt over low heat, being careful not to burn the chocolate. When melted, add sugar and cream and stir until incorporated. Cook until it reaches a simmer; reduce heat, and cook 5 minutes until slightly thick. Stir in Kahlúa. Remove and chill. Spoon over Espresso Ice Cream. Can add 1 teaspoon more Kahlúa to each serving. Yields 1 quart.

THE TROUTDALE DINING ROOM'S CHINESE-STYLE POACHED RAINBOW TROUT

water

1 bunch scallions

5 slices fresh ginger

2 14-ounce fresh trout,
   heads on

salt to taste

7 tablespoons peanut oil

1 tablespoon sesame oil

4 tablespoons Chinese soy
   sauce

Fill large skillet with water to cover trout by one inch. Bring water to boil with a few scallions cut lengthwise (3 inches) and in half. Add 2 to 3 slices ginger, the size of a quarter, and simmer 10 minutes. Meanwhile, cut remaining scallions the same way and slice 2-inch lengths of ginger into thin matchsticks. Place with cleaned trouts (heads on), and immerse in salted water with remaining scallions and ginger. Cover, reducing heat to a bare simmer and poach for 8 minutes. After 4 minutes, put oils in a small pan and heat to smoking. Remove trout and place on platter, covering each with ginger and scallions. Drizzle each with heated oil, and pour a good quality Chinese soy sauce over the trout. Serves 2.

HOTEL ROANOKE
Roanoke

HOTEL ROANOKE

My friend Bev advised me to order the Monte Cristo if lunching at the Hotel Roanoke, describing the dish as "the best" she'd ever eaten. I took her advice and completely agree. I also sampled the Peanut Soup and Spoonbread, and believe these culinary feats also must have contributed to the Regency Room Restaurant's four-star rating. Although I'd planned to have just one bite of the Black Forest Cake, there is no such thing as just one bite of chef Heinz Schlegel's concoction. I ate the whole thing, and it was worth the extra ten miles on my exercycle.

Judging by the other goodies I tried, including the Mariner Salad for dieters, a trip to the Regency Room for any meal is worthwhile. Unless pianist Van Cliburn is staying there. On the virtuoso's last visit, he started water running in the bathtub and then became sidetracked playing a Bach sonata. As luck decreed, the tub overflowed, seeping through the floor and drizzling down the crystal chandeliers onto guests in the dining room. Eventually, one guest did get up from a damp, gold velvet Louis XV chair and amble through the Georgian columns to alert someone.

Besides the food, what I appreciated most was the ambiance at this century-old, Tudor-style hotel. It's a working merger of gracious elegance and contemporary lifestyles. On the main level, past the inlaid marble-floored lobby, is the Oval Room. The ceiling fresco of billowing clouds blends with a blue and rose-colored carpet, woven in China.

Yet a young, energetic attitude emerges, even amid the grandeur. Shifting to the basement, you'll find such "unwinding" rooms as the Ad Lib Night Club, which features jazz musicians, or the Whistlestop Lounge. This room actually commemorates the reason for the hotel's existence. The hotel originally was built by the Norfolk and Western Railroad in order to give Big Lick, as Roanoke was known in 1882, a grand hotel. That scale has not tipped—it is still a grand hotel.

The Hotel Roanoke is located in downtown Roanoke on North Jefferson Street. Meals are served daily. Monday through Saturday, breakfast is served from 7:00 a.m. until 11:00 a.m.; lunch is served from 11:30 a.m. until 2:30 p.m.; and dinner is from 5:00 p.m. until 11:00 p.m. On Sunday, breakfast is served from 7:00 a.m. until 10:30 a.m.; lunch is from 11:30 a.m. until 3:00 p.m.; and dinner is served from 4:00 p.m. until 10:00 p.m. For reservations (recommended) call (703) 343-6992.

HOTEL ROANOKE'S PEANUT SOUP

½ stick of butter
¼ cup diced onion
1 branch celery, diced
1½ tablespoons flour
1 quart chicken broth or
   stock

½ pound peanut butter
1½ teaspoons celery salt
½ teaspoon salt
½ tablespoon lemon juice
¼ cup ground peanuts

Melt butter in skillet and sauté onion and celery until translucent. Add flour and mix well. Add hot chicken stock and cook for a half hour. Remove from stove, strain, and add peanut butter, celery salt, salt and lemon juice. Just before serving, sprinkle soup with ground peanuts. Serves 10, ½-cup portions.

HOTEL ROANOKE'S SPOONBREAD

1½ cups cornmeal
1⅓ teaspoons salt
1 teaspoon sugar
1½ cups boiling water

½ stick butter, melted
5 eggs
2 cups milk
1 teaspoon baking powder

Mix cornmeal, salt and sugar together and scald with boiling water. Add melted butter. Beat eggs and add milk to eggs. Combine the two mixtures and add baking powder. Pour into greased baking pan and bake 30 to 40 minutes at 350 degrees. Serves 10.

11

HOTEL ROANOKE'S STEAK DIANE

4 3-ounce center-cut fillets,
  thinly sliced
¼ cup chopped onion
¼ cup mushrooms
1 ounce brandy

Worcestershire and steak
  sauces to taste
salt, pepper and dry
  mustard to taste
2 ounces red wine

Sauté the meat, onion and mushrooms together. Flame with brandy, season with Worcestershire and steak sauces. Add other seasonings to taste and simmer five minutes in red wine. Serves 2.

HOTEL ROANOKE'S GERMAN POTATO SALAD

4 cups cooked, sliced
  potatoes
¾ cup fried bacon, chopped
⅓ to ½ cup bacon drippings
1 large, finely chopped
  onion

salt and pepper to taste
½ cup chicken stock
1½ cups hot water
⅛ cup chopped chives
½ cup vinegar

Combine the above ingredients and heat (may be served cold). Serves 8.

SAM SNEAD'S TAVERN
Hot Springs

SAM SNEAD'S TAVERN

This sporty tavern is definitely a "letting-go" type of place. A few years ago, Hot Springs' famous son, professional golfer Sam Snead, took this old bank and transformed it into a casual club. If you know little about golf before dropping into Sam's, you won't leave in the same condition. Not only did Mrs. Snead make the downstairs into a museum of Sam's vast accomplishments, but the menu, in golf lingo, explains Sam's history, along with that of the building.

When the building was constructed in 1920, it cost $15,000, and the massive vault that you see standing wide open as you enter was purchased for $7,000. The vault, which now holds the tavern's wine, is considered an engineering marvel. The door alone weighs 2,000 pounds, but is balanced so that it can be closed with one hand. The door locks are set by a timing mechanism to open at a specific time only. I'm told that in an emergency, the only alternative would be to blow open the doors, which would, consequently, blow open the building. So far, nobody has needed a bottle of wine that badly.

Maybe it's because the tavern offers such an enticing variety of mixed drinks—everything from a Buzz Bomb to a Piña Colada with vanilla ice cream. I favor the latter, which is served to children minus the rum.

For lunch, I went for the Mexiskins. Hot, hot, and hot, so I cooled the recipe down a tad for you. My main course was their Hickory Smoked Ribs, which, yes, are definitely in the finger lickin' category.

If you are thinking of something not quite so spicy or calorically powerful, you might want their Sunshine Salad topped with sunflower seeds. At dinner, you couldn't go wrong with Allegheny Trout. Just ask them to broil it in wine for you. After dinner, try one of their international coffees.

The restaurant has a Mobil three-star rating, and the promise of their motto, ". . . where you can bank on great food and cocktails," is, in my opinion, amply fulfilled.

Sam Snead's Tavern is located at 1 Main Street in Hot Springs. Meals are served daily from 11:30 a.m. until 9:00 p.m., Sunday through Thursday and from 11:30 a.m. until 10:00 p.m. on Friday and Saturday. For reservations (recommended) call (703) 839-2828.

SAM SNEAD'S TAVERN'S CHICKEN CURRY BROCCOLI SOUP

1 3- to 4-pound chicken	2 tablespoons butter
3 quarts chicken stock or broth	¾ cup uncooked rice
2 bunches broccoli	2 16-ounce cans of tomatoes
1½ onions	1 tablespoon red pepper
2 stalks celery	2 tablespoons curry powder
1 carrot	dash of sage
	salt and pepper to taste

Cook chicken in stock or broth about an hour and a half over medium heat. When meat easily separates from the bone, remove chicken, and let the stock simmer. Debone and discard skin as chicken is torn into bite-size pieces and set aside. Destem broccoli, cutting and separating flowerettes. Add chicken and broccoli to simmering stock. Mince onions; slice celery on the diagonal; shred or dice carrot. Sauté onions, celery and carrot in butter until translucent. Add sautéed vegetables to stock along with rice, tomatoes and spices. Simmer for 45 minutes. Serves 16.

Note: Recipe may be divided in half using 2 pounds of chicken parts.

SAM SNEAD'S TAVERN'S HOUSE DRESSING

6 tablespoons honey	1 tablespoon celery seeds
¾ cup cider vinegar	1 tablespoon poppy seeds
1½ cups salad oil	½ tablespoon ground mustard
¼ small onion, minced	½ teaspoon paprika
1 tablespoon parsley	

Put all ingredients in blender and blend on high speed until creamy. Yields about 3 cups.

SAM SNEAD'S TAVERN'S MEXISKINS

2 large baked potatoes
4 ounces hamburger
2 tablespoons onions, diced
2 tablespoons green
  peppers, diced
1 tablespoon jalapeño
  peppers, diced

2 tablespoons tomatoes,
  chopped
2 teaspoons chili powder
3 ounces Cheddar cheese,
  shredded
3 ounces Monterey Jack,
  shredded

Slice potatoes in quarters and scoop out to ¼ inch from skin. Cook hamburger until pink disappears. Add diced onions, both varieties of peppers and chopped tomatoes, sautéing until translucent. Add chili powder, mixing well. Fill skins with mixture and top evenly with shredded cheeses. Place under broiler until cheese melts. Serves 2.

SAM SNEAD'S TAVERN'S PIÑA COLADA

2½ cups chunk pineapple
  and juice
½ cup creme of coconut

2 heavy pinches shredded
  coconut

Blend pineapple, creme of coconut and shredded coconut in blender. Mix is enough for 12 servings.

¼ cup blended mix
1½ ounces light rum
1 scoop vanilla ice cream
1½ scoops ice

½ teaspoon shredded
  coconut
1 cherry

Place ¼ cup of prepared pineapple mix in blender and add rum, ice cream and ice. Blend until frothy. Pour into glass and top with shredded coconut and a cherry. Serves 1.

THE HOMESTEAD
Hot Springs

THE HOMESTEAD   In the early 1900s you were admitted to The Homestead only if society had recorded your name in its Blue Book. The story goes that two dowagers were rocking on the veranda, and one of them said, "Those people coming up the walk aren't in the Book. Why would The Homestead admit them?"

"Maybe The Homestead needs the money," replied the other.

"Well, *really*, couldn't they just send the money, I mean, must they come?"

Ah, yes, why spoil life for the aristocracy? They had been coming to partake of the curative hot springs and mountain air since 1766 when the first inn was built. Nevertheless, after Pearl Harbor, the State Department chose The Homestead as the ideal place of internment for the Japanese diplomatic staff. Since geography virtually cloisters the inn in a crevice of the Allegheny Mountains, the staff was protected in luxury for the first months of the war.

Although war and changing social mores did disturb this playground for the "Blue Bookers," old world manners still remain. For the first time in my tour of restaurants, I saw a maître d' slide a silver crumber over the white linen tablecloth to collect the luncheon crumbs before dessert was served. I was so fascinated watching the crumber glide around the fresh bouquet of tulips that I spilled my hot tea. So much for my admittance to Blue Book society.

Seriously, though, my Southern lunch of Short Ribs, delicately cooked with a light sauce, was really very good, and I especially enjoyed their preparation of zucchini. I found the Raspberry Poppy Seed Dressing to be so exceptional that I went back into their cavernous kitchen to get the recipe for you. I also toured the pastry kitchen, snacking all the way down into the wine cellar, which has a selection to please any royal taste.

There are many dining rooms in this majestic Georgian brick, five-star resort, but I felt fortunate to lunch in the

Regency Room. Its dance floor is partitioned with Corinthian columns, giving the room an atrium effect. The Homestead has been called a social spa, Versailles and a palace. To me it was a castle with an underground moat of bubbling hot springs, where I had a wonderful time.

The Homestead is located on Route 220 in Hot Springs. Breakfast is served daily from 7:30 a.m. until 9:30 a.m., and lunch is from 12:30 p.m. until 2:00 p.m. Dinner is served from 7:00 p.m. with the last seating at 8:30 p.m. For reservations (recommended) call (703) 839-5500.

THE HOMESTEAD'S RASPBERRY POPPY SEED DRESSING

1½ cups sugar	2 tablespoons onion juice
⅔ cup raspberry vinegar	2 cups vegetable oil
1 teaspoon English mustard	3 tablespoons poppy seeds
1 teaspoon salt	

Mix everything together in a blender except oil and poppy seeds. Blend well. Add oil slowly until dressing reaches thick consistency. Add poppy seeds and blend. Serve over salad. Yields 1 quart.

THE HOMESTEAD'S CREAM OF WATERCRESS

1 bunch of watercress	¼ stalk of celery, sliced
6 tablespoons butter	1 small leek, diced
4 tablespoons chicken stock	1½ ounces flour
1 small onion, chopped	1 cup half and half

Pick the leaves from a large bunch of watercress. Chop leaves and simmer in 2 tablespoons butter and 2 tablespoons chicken stock for 5 minutes and set aside. Cut up coarsely the stems of the remaining watercress and mix with onion, celery and leek. Simmer in 2 tablespoons of butter and 2 tablespoons chicken stock for 30 minutes. Stir into a combined mixture of 2 tablespoons melted butter and 1½ ounces

19

flour. Bring to a boil. Add half and half, stirring constantly, and simmer for 10 minutes. Strain. Add the precooked watercress leaves to the liquid. Season to taste with salt. If too thick, add more cream or milk. Serve hot. Serves 4.

THE HOMESTEAD'S ROAST TURKEY "MARCO POLO"

2 bunches fresh broccoli	**Mornay Sauce**
12 slices roasted turkey	**Parmesan cheese to taste**

Boil broccoli until barely tender. Place broccoli in greased casserole dish and cover with sliced, hot turkey so that only tops of broccoli show. Cover completely with Mornay Sauce (recipe below). Sprinkle Parmesan cheese on top and place under broiler until golden brown. Serves 4.

Mornay Sauce:

3 tablespoons butter	**salt to taste**
2 tablespoons flour	**white pepper to taste**
2 cups milk, heated	**¼ cup ham, julienned**
¼ cup grated Parmesan cheese	**¼ cup mushrooms, julienned**

Melt butter in pan, add flour to make roux. Set aside to cool for 2 to 3 minutes. Add hot milk, stir until boiling, then simmer for 5 to 10 minutes. (Add more milk to thin if necessary.) Add cheese, salt, pepper, ham and mushrooms. Simmer until cheese melts and mushrooms are heated.

WATERWHEEL RESTAURANT
THE INN AT GRISTMILL SQUARE
Warm Springs

WATERWHEEL RESTAURANT

Nestled in the valley of the Allegheny Mountains is the Inn at Gristmill Square. My first impression was "I know that painting" because the setting looks like a nineteenth century work of art in the Hudson River genre. Modern cars and telephone wires reminded me that I hadn't slipped into a time warp.

The large, twenty-foot waterwheel on the side of the red wooden restaurant was once powered by a ninety-eight-degree creek heated from the igneous rocks of the famous warm springs. The wheel can still turn just as it did back in 1771 when miller Jacob Butler ground his cornmeal for spoonbread and hoe cakes. Today, at the converted Waterwheel Restaurant, your palate will experience far more sophisticated fare.

Inside, the restaurant's décor has an inviting, posh, country look. The wide plank walls have been whitewashed and hold candle lanterns which cast a soft, unobtrusive light.

Before dining, you can go into the gravel-floored wine cellar and select from wines displayed amidst the mechanism that once powered the waterwheel. Back upstairs, some of the mill's original tools, such as grinding presses, continue to stand where they were installed. Because you are in an old mill, the equipment does not seem out of place with tables set with pink linen tablecloths, fresh flowers and wine-colored china.

I had been overindulging so I chose their Trout broiled in garlic and wine. Before the entrée, a relish tray of Marinated Vegetables was served. This course was followed by a fresh green salad accompanied by a small loaf of freshly baked bread on its own cutting board. The Trout dish was decidedly one of the best I've ever tasted. If, however, you don't need to cut calories, your interest might lie in an appetizer of Seviche followed by Honey Mustard Glazed Spareribs, Chicken Tarragon or a French preparation of Duck.

For dessert I tried one bite of their Apple Cake with Rum Sauce and one bite of their Chocolate Mousse. After dinner I visited their quaint pub, named after the heroic pioneer

Simon Kenton. I had a marvelous liqueur-embellished coffee and thought that if I had been the rating party from Mobil, this restaurant and charming inn would have netted five stars instead of four.

The Waterwheel Restaurant in the Inn at Gristmill Square is located in Warm Springs. Dinner is served from 6:30 p.m. until 9:00 p.m., Tuesday through Saturday. Sunday buffet is served from noon until 4:00 p.m. For reservations (recommended) call (703) 839-2231.

WATERWHEEL RESTAURANT'S SCALLOP SEVICHE A LA TALLITIENNE

1½ pounds fresh scallops
2 tablespoons olive oil
1 teaspoon salt
3 tablespoons chopped
  parsley

½ cup strained lime juice
⅛ teaspoon minced garlic
1 tablespoon freshly
  crushed black
  peppercorns

Combine all ingredients in a shallow ceramic or glass bowl and chill, covered, for 3 hours (or overnight). Stir occasionally. Serve in a small cocktail glass or a small, carved out pineapple. Serves 4.

WATERWHEEL RESTAURANT'S AMARETTO SOUFFLÉ

1 cup sugar
½ cup water
9 egg yolks
¼ cup sifted powdered
  sugar

½ cup amaretto
1½ teaspoons vanilla
¾ quart of heavy cream,
  whipped until stiff

Mix sugar and water and bring to a boil for 15 to 20 minutes. In a mixer, mix yolks until a ribbon shows (pale yellow) and add sifted powdered sugar. Fold egg mixture into sugar water slowly. Cool to room temperature. Add amaretto, vanilla and whipped cream; mix. Cover and refrigerate until chilled. Serve immediately. Serves 10.

WATERWHEEL RESTAURANT'S HONEY MUSTARD GLAZED SPARERIBS

2 cups orange juice
¼ cup soy sauce
3 garlic cloves, crushed
¼ teaspoon ginger (fresh or ground)
¼ cup grated orange peel
1 cup pure honey

3 teaspoons hot mustard (or Dijon-style)
16 pork spareribs, boiled until tender
rice (follow package directions)
chopped parsley

Mix all ingredients well except rice and spareribs. Pour mixture over ribs and cover with foil. Marinate overnight. The next day, broil ribs in same juice until crisp and let set in warm oven (375 degrees) for 15 minutes. Serve with rice sprinkled with chopped parsley. Serves 4.

WATERWHEEL RESTAURANT'S CHICKEN IN TARRAGON CREAM SAUCE

whole chicken, skinned, cut up and lightly floured
¼ cup butter
¼ cup oil
4 large shallots, peeled and finely chopped
½ cup white wine
2 cups chicken stock
¼ cup fresh cream
¼ cup chives, chopped

1½ cups fresh mushrooms, sliced
¼ cup brandy
½ teaspoon tarragon (fresh or dried)
¼ cup fresh parsley, finely chopped
salt and pepper to taste
rice or potatoes

Sauté chicken parts in ¼ cup soft butter plus ¼ cup of oil until golden. Put aside. Sauté shallots in the same pan and stir with wooden spoon until light yellow. Glaze with white wine; add chicken stock. Reduce heat. Add cream, chives and mushrooms and stir. Add chicken parts to sauce; cook over low flame for 15 minutes. Add brandy, tarragon, parsley, salt and pepper. Cook 5 more minutes. Serve with rice or parsleyed potatoes. Serves 4.

WARM SPRINGS INN AND RESTAURANT
Warm Springs

**WARM SPRINGS INN
AND RESTAURANT**

Nothing, but nothing, smells more inviting than an apple pie in the oven. The early spring morning that I breakfasted at Warm Springs, that aroma tinged the air.

Because I was trying to get a cross section of the restaurant's menu, I wound up eating a rather odd breakfast. It was a wonderful Cheese Omelet, a spicy dish of Sauerkraut Relish and, you guessed it, a smidgen of that aromatic Apple Pie. The two latter items weren't on the breakfast menu, but I wanted to try them for the benefit of the recipes.

The dining room tables and windows are full of potted flowers grown by Grandmother Routier, the wife of the late Edmund Routier who first came to America as The Homestead's pastry chef. The Routier's granddaughter, Michelle, told me that more than thirty years ago, her grandparents converted a 1791 jail and courthouse into this inn and restaurant.

The lobby, which once served as the courthouse, is decorated with white wicker settees comfortably arranged around the fireplace. There is no designer touch to the room. It is simply a reflection of the family's interests. Perhaps the most remarkable items in the lobby are Chef Routier's paintings, which are done in the medium of bakers' cocoa. The paintings of Winston Churchill and friends resemble softly etched pastels, but one that had a more abstract quality seems to have suffered from its proximity to the fireplace, which caused the cocoa to melt. Apparently, to cook with cocoa and have those culinary masterpieces consumed is a compliment, but it is a different story when the function of the masterpiece is to hang on the wall.

The current generation of Routiers do not, however, consider their foods to be masterpieces, just simple mountain fare with French overtones.

Roast Beef is the favorite dish, with Virginia Ham a very close second. For dieters, a low-calorie plate of Grilled Lean Hamburger served with fruits and cottage cheese is available.

There is a small but interesting wine list, selected to complement specific dishes, plus a wide assortment of beers.

Although people no longer visit Warm Springs for the baths, which turned out to lack curative powers, they continue to come every season for the warm hospitality and food at this charming old inn snuggled in the lap of the Allegheny Mountains.

The Warm Springs Inn and Restaurant is located in Warm Springs at Highways 220 and 39. Meals are served daily from March 15 through November 30. Breakfast is served from 7:30 a.m. until 9:30 a.m., and dinner is served from 6:30 p.m. until 8:30 p.m. Lunch is served on Sunday only, from 12:30 p.m. until 2:00 p.m. For reservations (preferred) call (703) 839–5351.

WARM SPRINGS INN'S APPLE PIE

Dough:

2¼ cups flour	¾ cup shortening, room
2 tablespoons sugar	temperature
1 teaspoon salt	5 to 6 tablespoons ice water

Sift flour, sugar and salt together. Cut in shortening with knives. Sprinkle ice water into mixture, 1 tablespoon at a time, and work mixture until it sticks together when pressed with a fork. Form a ball of dough and chill in the refrigerator for at least 15 minutes. On lightly floured board, roll out dough in a circle, working from the center outward. Place in 9-inch, deep pie pan and press against the edges.

Apple Pie Filling:

6 small tart apples	1 cup brown sugar
cold water flavored with	1 teaspoon cinnamon
1 teaspoon vinegar or	6 tablespoons butter, cubed
lemon juice (enough	
water to cover apples)	

Peel and slice the apples and set aside in cold water flavored with a teaspoon of vinegar or lemon juice. Place apples

27

in pie crust. Mix sugar and cinnamon and cover apples completely with mixture. Dot the cubes of butter on top. Bake at 350 degrees for 45 minutes. Yields 1 pie.

WARM SPRINGS INN'S SAUERKRAUT RELISH

1 quart shredded kraut
  (drained)
1 green pepper, chopped
1 cup celery, diced

1 onion, chopped
1 small can pimientos,
  chopped

Mix ingredients in bowl and set aside.

½ cup vinegar
1½ cups sugar

½ cup oil

Mix these ingredients together and pour over vegetables. Toss well, cover, and let stand in refrigerator overnight. Yields 1½ quarts.

WARM SPRINGS INN'S CORN BREAD

6 tablespoons sugar
6 tablespoons shortening
2 eggs
1¼ cups flour
½ teaspoon baking powder

1 teaspoon salt
1¼ cups yellow cornmeal
1 cup sweet milk and 1 cup
  buttermilk, combined

Mix sugar, shortening and eggs together until completely mixed. Mix flour, baking powder and salt. Alternately add cornmeal, milk and dry ingredients to the sugar/egg mixture until it reaches thick consistency. Place in a 11-inch by 7½-inch greased pan and bake at 425 degrees until brown, about 10 to 12 minutes. Yields 15 squares.

THE VICTORIAN RESTAURANT
Danville

THE VICTORIAN
RESTAURANT

Built in 1883, the architecture of the red brick Victorian Restaurant reminds you of the dignity of that bygone era. Once inside you find a dichotomy of the past and present comfortably juxtaposed.

Upon entering the stately foyer, you walk through carved walnut doors inset with etched, satin glass. You are simultaneously struck by the elaborate interior and the upbeat wailing of what the proprietors call "soft rock and roll."

I was seated in the front parlor beside an utterly magnificent black marble fireplace. I've never seen such intricate inlays of gold with multicolored marble. Ceiling medallions are enhanced by ornately carved moldings. For lunch I partook of a Danville favorite—the Steak and Cheese Sandwich. I so enjoyed this unusual preparation that I went into the kitchen and learned how to make it. While there, I also sampled their special barbecue sauce known as Rocket Fuel. One hearty taste and it took a whole Pepsi to extinguish my fire. If you are going to barbecue, this is great to use for steaks, chicken and even shrimp dishes.

When stopping by for dinner, a delicious suggestion is their Barbecued Spare Ribs. If you are watching your calories, you could have the Broiled Flounder or Scallops.

You will be surprised by the bar's interesting and potent assortment of cocktails. I have secured three recipes for your home sampling. Go easy though, they pack a wallop.

This beautifully restored home, built by Thomas J. Lee, has many stories to tell, but the one that flagged my fancy concerns the Jones' adopted daughter's pet parrot. It was named, appropriately enough, Polly.

Old-timers say that Polly had free run of the house and yard. She conversed, snatched ice cream cones from passersby and became a legendary fixture in Danville. Thus, when Polly passed on to parrot glory, a special coffin was built for her and an actual funeral service was held. The local paper's obituary column reported that the service was swamped with mourners.

Well, I suppose it's not often you have the opportunity to experience a parrot funeral. But you can experience the Victorian, and that's a treat you shouldn't miss.

The Victorian Restaurant is located at 913 North Main Street in Danville. Meals are served from 11:30 a.m. until 11:00 p.m., Tuesday through Friday, and from 5:00 p.m. until 11:00 p.m. Saturday. For reservations (preferred for larger groups) call (804) 799–4268.

THE VICTORIAN RESTAURANT'S STEAK AND CHEESE SANDWICH

8 ounces steak or roast beef, cooked
6 heaping tablespoons onion, sliced in one-inch pieces
1 tablespoon butter
4 slices Provolone cheese
2 hoagie rolls
mayonnaise to taste, about 1 to 2 teaspoons
4 teaspoons canned mushrooms, sliced

Using leftover steak or freshly cooked roast beef, slice thin and set aside. Steam sliced onion in butter until transparent. Split hoagie buns and place in oven at about 250 degrees to warm. Remove and spread mayonnaise on both sides; add mushrooms, sliced cheese and meat slices. Top with steamed onions. Serves 2.

THE VICTORIAN RESTAURANT'S ROCKET FUEL

3 tablespoons salt
3½ tablespoons black pepper
3½ tablespoons garlic powder
½ tablespoon chili powder
½ teaspoon cayenne
2 cups catsup
2 small peppers from Texas Pete, cut up
1½ teaspoons juice from Texas Pete liquid
¼ cup vinegar
2 teaspoons Worcestershire sauce

Place all dry ingredients together in a bowl and mix until well incorporated. Add liquid ingredients and peppers slowly until thick consistency is reached. Serves 6 to 8.

Note: Larger quantities can be made and frozen for later use. Always taste while doubling recipes as some ingredients need to either be increased or decreased, depending on how hot and spicy you want the barbecue to be.

THE VICTORIAN RESTAURANT'S BRICK LAYER

1 ounce light rum	1½ ounces orange juice
1 ounce dark rum	½ ounce grain alcohol, to
½ ounce 151-proof rum	float on top
½ ounce grenadine	orange or lime wedge

Combine all ingredients except grain alcohol and garnish. Stir to thoroughly blend flavors. Pour over ice. Float grain alcohol on top and garnish with an orange or lime wedge. Serves 1.

THE VICTORIAN RESTAURANT'S PINEAPPLE BOMB

1½ ounces bourbon	6 to 8 ounces pineapple
1½ ounces amaretto	juice

Combine all ingredients and stir to blend liquids thoroughly. Pour over ice in two 6- to 8-ounce glasses. Serves 2.

THE VICTORIAN RESTAURANT'S SOUTH PACIFIC

½ ounce light rum	½ ounce Creme de Noyaux
½ ounce dark rum	1½ ounces pineapple juice
½ ounce 151-proof rum	1½ ounces orange juice
½ ounce peach brandy	1½ ounces sour mix
½ ounce apricot brandy	

Mix all ingredients, stirring well to blend all flavors, and serve over ice. Serves 1 or 2.

THE EAGLE
Lynchburg

THE EAGLE

The standard joke at The Eagle is that each of their recipes begins with, "First, you melt a half pound of butter . . ." Not so. You only assume everything is rich in calories because it is all so scrumptious. Dieters can have their Spinach, Roast Beef, Mushroom Salad or Broiled Seafood and still enjoy delicious food, guilt free.

This sturdy, old 1915 bank building, designed in the style of Beaux Arts architecture, was erected with reinforced cement walls and floor that are two feet thick. The interior has been decorated to resemble what else but an old bank. The chairs are exactly like the comfortable and very identifiable old wooden chairs I sat in as a child when visiting the bank with my grandmother. The ceiling is a one-of-a-kind plaster and tin in bas-relief with an exquisite crystal chandelier that can be seen from the street through arched windows. I think banks should exude an aura of secure prestige, and The Eagle, without being stuffy, does just that.

The white linen tablecloths are set with fan-shaped napkins, and a fresh red carnation provides the right touch at each table. It's specifically the kind of place you'd want to take a business client for lunch or dinner. Because it is located downtown in the business district, management has pridefully decorated the walls with the original newspaper clippings of Lynchburg's business establishments, many of which are still open.

Relaxing before dinner with classical music, I enjoyed a rum and cream Ramos Fizz Cocktail, followed by a homemade tangy Tomato Soup. The salad is called Premier and I'd agree that it, along with the dressing, is definitely first class. I then chose their Cornish Game Hen stuffed with rice. It was tender and moist with a subtle sauce that I found easy to duplicate later in my own kitchen.

Their wine list, like their array of liqueurs, includes just about anything you might fancy to complement your meal. For safe keeping, spirits are locked away upstairs in the vault.

For dessert you are beset by decisions, but you won't go wrong with either the French Silk Pie or the Almond Eagle.

The Eagle is located at 11th and Main Streets in Lynchburg. Lunch is served from 11:30 a.m. until 3:00 p.m., Monday through Friday; dinner is served from 6:00 p.m. until 10:00 p.m., Monday through Saturday. For reservations (recommended for weekend dining and parties of four or more) call (804) 846-3898.

THE EAGLE'S CORNISH GAME HEN

4 cornish game hens

Stuffing:

1 cup uncooked brown rice	**1 teaspoon thyme**
2 to 3 tablespoons butter	**¼ teaspoon minced garlic**
¼ cup chopped onions	**½ teaspoon black pepper**
¼ cup chopped mushrooms	**1 teaspoon salt**
3 tablespoons green peppers, minced	**1 raw egg**

Cook rice according to package directions and set aside. In skillet, melt butter and sauté vegetables. Add seasonings and cooked rice, mixing thoroughly. Add egg to thicken mixture. Wash cavities of hens and stuff. Tie ends with string or clamps to hold stuffing inside.

Basting Sauce:

½ cup olive oil	**½ teaspoon pepper**
1 teaspoon tarragon	**1 teaspoon rosemary**
1 teaspoon basil	**1 teaspoon lemon peel, grated**
juice of half a lemon	
1 teaspoon salt	**1 clove garlic, crushed**

Blend all ingredients together until thoroughly mixed. Place hens on roasting pan and baste with sauce every 15 to 20 minutes. Cook in 400-degree oven. Insert meat thermometer to test. Depending on size, cook approximately 1 hour. Serves 4.

35

THE EAGLE'S STEAK SCAMPI AU POIVRE

12 large prawns
1½ pounds beef tenderloin
    or top sirloin
3 tablespoons cracked
    peppercorns
4 tablespoons butter
2 tablespoons cognac (or
    brandy)

½ cup chopped scallions
1 cup sour cream
1 tablespoon salt
rice or pasta (follow
    package directions)

Clean and devein prawns. Slice beef ⅛ inch thick across grain and press half of peppercorns into strips. Heat butter in skillet over medium-high heat and add beef and sear on both sides. Remove from pan and add prawns. Cook about 2 minutes until prawns curl and turn pink. Remove prawns and deglaze pan with cognac. Add remaining peppercorns and scallions, cooking for 1 minute. Stir in sour cream and salt. Arrange beef strips on heated plate, garnish with prawns, and drizzle with sauce from skillet. Serve with rice or pasta. Serves 4.

THE EAGLE'S FRENCH SILK PIE

½ cup butter (room
    temperature)
¾ cup sugar
1½ squares unsweetened
    chocolate

4 eggs
1 teaspoon vanilla
1 baked graham cracker pie
    crust
1 cup whipped cream

Cream butter and sugar together. Melt chocolate in top of double boiler and add to creamed mixture, blending thoroughly. Add one egg and beat for five minutes; add additional eggs one at a time, beating each for five minutes. Add vanilla and blend into mixture. Pour into 9-inch baked pie shell and refrigerate to set. May freeze if desired. Before serving, top with whipped cream. Yields 1 pie.

JOSEPH NICHOLS TAVERN
Lynchburg

JOSEPH NICHOLS TAVERN

The fact that the 1815 Joseph Nichols Tavern is in healthy operation attests to the supportive community in Lynchburg. When the brick, Federal-style structure, which had become known as the Western Hotel, was slated for the demolition crews in 1975, a committed group of townspeople fought and won the battle to preserve this important page of Lynchburg's history.

During the tavern's early years, it was a thriving ordinary, or inn, and rumor has it that Thomas Jefferson slept here on his way from Monticello to his summer home in Poplar Forest. Then sometime after 1840 it served as one of the many brothels that were particularly popular with out-of-towners in those days.

In subsequent years it saw its ups and downs, turning from brothel to rooming house to private home, and finally to an abandoned haven for transients.

Today, through the unceasing efforts of the Restoration and Housing Corporation, the upstairs has been made into apartments, and the downstairs has become a dinner theater with a growing patronage.

Guests dine in a large room decorated with two colonial blue fireplaces and eat at large, linen-covered, family-style tables on a set menu that changes weekly. The large table gathering fosters a spirit of camaraderie among guests who perhaps have not met before coming to the tavern.

It's rather hard to pinpoint the type of cuisine, but it has a Southern influence without being what is known as "country cooking." The evening that I visited, the menu offered Southern Peanut Soup, a unique Fruit Salad, Stuffed Cabbage Rolls, Pineapple Muffins and Carrot Cake for dessert. I liked the diversity of the menu and was particularly fond of the Pineapple Muffins. Although licensing does not permit the sale of alcoholic beverages, guests may bring their own bottles of wine.

After dinner, guests move across the foyer to the room that the Joseph Nichols Players have converted into a theater.

Broadway plays are the usual entertainment, but local play-wrights have quite successfully produced their own works here, the most notable being *Lynchburg, Then and Now*, which is scheduled to reopen on Lynchburg's birthday in 1986. Don't wait until then to enjoy a delicious and entertaining evening at the tavern.

The Joseph Nichols Tavern is located at Madison and 5th Streets in Lynchburg. Dinner is served at 6:30 p.m., Friday and Saturday, except in December and August when the tavern closes. For reservations (required) call (804) 845-6153.

JOSEPH NICHOLS TAVERN'S STUFFED CABBAGE ROLLS

1 large head of cabbage	½ teaspoon thyme
1½ pounds ground chuck	1 teaspoon salt
1 onion, chopped	½ teaspoon pepper
1 garlic clove, finely chopped	½ cup uncooked rice (boil 3 to 5 minutes)

Cut core out of cabbage and pull off outer leaves; wilt remaining cabbage leaves in boiling water about 5 minutes. Shred remaining head of cabbage. Combine all other ingredients. Make 1- to 2-inch balls out of meat mixture and roll each in wilted cabbage leaf. Serves 4 to 6.

Sauce:

1 16-ounce can tomato sauce	1 tablespoon Worcestershire sauce
1 rounded teaspoon brown sugar	1 teaspoon caraway seeds

Mix tomato sauce with brown sugar, Worcestershire sauce and caraway seeds. Line bottom of a greased 13-inch by 9-inch pan with shredded, uncooked cabbage. Place cabbage rolls on top and cover with sauce. Bake in a 350-degree oven for 1½ hours. Serves 4 to 6.

JOSEPH NICHOLS TAVERN'S BLUEBERRY MUFFINS

2 cups plain flour
½ cup sugar
1 teaspoon salt
2 teaspoons baking powder
1 cup milk

1 egg
⅓ cup oil
1 cup blueberries (frozen, fresh or canned)

Mix flour, sugar, salt and baking powder. Combine milk, egg and oil and add to dry ingredients. Fold in drained blueberries. Pour into greased muffin tins. Bake at 400 degrees for 15 to 20 minutes. Yields 12 to 15 muffins.

JOSEPH NICHOLS TAVERN'S SALAD AND DRESSING

Salad:
1 head Boston lettuce
1 grapefruit, sectioned

1 orange, peeled
12 slices pimientos

Place lettuce leaves on four plates and add 3 to 4 sections of grapefruit, 2 orange slices and 3 pimientos to each. Pour dressing over top. Serves 4.

Dressing:
⅓ cup oil
¼ cup white wine vinegar
1 teaspoon oregano
2 teaspoons sugar

1 teaspoon salt
¼ teaspoon pepper
½ teaspoon parsley

Place all ingredients in blender and blend until mixed. Yields ⅔ cup.

THE RUTLEDGE INN
Amherst

THE RUTLEDGE INN

The Rutledge Inn is the kind of place you fantasize about popping into after skiing all day in the Alps. You know the type—rustic weathered walls, thick beams and moose heads hanging above stone fireplaces. It's a sturdy old inn where you close your eyes and see the movie camera pan across the room to catch James Bond nonchalantly removing his ski parka while crystals of snow fall outside.

I've noticed that they never seem to eat in those films; food is ordered and occasionally picked at, but never really eaten. I suppose eating doesn't lend enough action to sustain a thriller.

Back to reality. Guests, such as you and I, don't visit The Rutledge Inn to entrap spies. Nor do we pop in after skiing all day since the nearest ski area is miles away. We come because of the food and lodging.

This old inn was built in the early thirties as a hunting lodge. Arriving early afternoon, I went to my bedroom which, like the dining room, was a picture of quaintness. Swiss painted furniture, a cathedral ceiling, plus a view of the rolling landscape outside my window provided the right combination for a romantic interlude. Alone, but tucking this setting away for future reference, I went down to dinner.

Owners and chefs Urs and Michelle Gabathuler have brought their Swiss techniques of food preparation in the continental mode to appreciative gourmets at this romantic inn.

Noting that veal is their specialty, I ordered half entrées of their Veal Zurich and their Scallops Bombay. Both dishes are accompanied by a Potato Pancake and a very unusual German Salad of marinated carrots, cabbage and potatoes. Along with their Swiss Rolls, such unusual offerings aren't apt to be found elsewhere.

My waiter suggested a liebfraumilch, a suitable selection for my entrées, but you might prefer one of their subtler offerings.

The Swiss influence really shines when it comes to pastries and desserts. It's so hard to choose when you are presented with a pastry tray that places each entry in competition with the next. Obviously, Apple Strudel is going to be great, but how about Carrot Almond Cake? Superb!

On the other hand, if you feel the need to relax calorie consumption, you might lean toward their Dover Sole Watewska, poached in white wine. Pass up the pastries and enjoy a fruit dessert.

Whatever your dining choice or private fantasy, this inn will do nothing less than embellish your desires.

The Rutledge Inn is located on Highway 60 East in Amherst. Lunch is served from 11:30 a.m. until 2:30 p.m., and dinner is from 5:30 p.m. until 9:00 p.m., Tuesday through Friday. On Saturday, dinner is served from 5:00 p.m. until 9:00 p.m. Sunday brunch is from 11:30 a.m. until 2:30 p.m. For reservations (recommended) call (804) 946-5545.

THE RUTLEDGE INN'S CARROT ALMOND CAKE

5 egg yolks
2½ cups confectioners' sugar plus enough confectioners' sugar for top
1 tablespoon grated lemon peel
10½ ounces almonds, finely grated
3 carrots, finely grated

4 tablespoons sifted flour
1½ tablespoons cinnamon
pinch of salt
1 tablespoon baking powder
5 egg whites
2 tablespoons cherry brandy or rum
butter for greasing pan

Beat egg yolks, sugar and lemon peel with electric mixer until smooth. Add almonds and carrots to egg mixture and combine using a wooden spoon. Add flour, cinnamon, salt, and baking powder. Stir and combine. Beat egg whites until stiff and gently fold into mixture. Stir in cherry brandy. Grease a 9-inch by 13-inch cake pan liberally and pour in mixture. Bake at 350 degrees for 60 minutes or until toothpick comes out clean. Sprinkle with confectioners' sugar. Yields 1 cake.

THE RUTLEDGE INN'S SCALLOPS BOMBAY

1 pound sea scallops
salt and pepper to taste
½ teaspoon Worcestershire
   sauce
juice of one lemon
¾ teaspoon curry powder
⅔ cup shallots, chopped
3 tablespoons butter

2 tablespoons flour
1 cup Chablis
⅓ cup whipping cream
rice (follow package
   directions)
whipped cream rosettes
   (optional)

Place scallops into small bowl and marinate for thirty minutes or longer with salt, pepper, Worcestershire sauce, lemon juice and curry. In a large skillet, sauté shallots in butter until soft. Lift scallops with a slotted spoon, powder with flour, adding enough until marinade is mostly absorbed. Reduce heat to medium and add scallops to skillet. Sauté for 2 minutes, add Chablis, let simmer for 5 minutes or until scallops are almost done. Remove scallops and reduce wine by half. Return scallops to pan, add cream and stir lightly. Place scallops on bed of rice. If desired, garnish with whipped cream rosettes made with special pastry tip. Sprinkle with curry powder. Serves 4.

BUCKHORN INN
Churchville

BUCKHORN INN

From the Buckhorn Inn's upstairs veranda, which encircles the inn, the distant view of the Shenandoah Mountains became the most soothing moment of my day. Pastel blossoming dogwoods and lilacs polka-dotting the dusky landscape resembled the country quilt on my bed in the antique-appointed bedroom.

Feeling more at peace after my veranda visit, I descended the curving staircase that Stonewall Jackson and his wife Elinor had trod back in 1854 when they stayed at this inn. It seems that from 1800 to 1861 the Buckhorn Tavern, as it was then known, was a popular stop for stagecoaches carrying folks, such as the Jacksons, who were on their way to the famed hot springs in Bath County.

Later, when the Civil War engulfed this serene territory, the Buckhorn became a hospital for the soldiers who were wounded during the Battle of McDowell. With the many changes that followed the war, the tavern became a dance hall and gambling house where it is believed a gambler was either murdered or committed suicide in what is now a passageway to the kitchen. The Buckhorn employees told me they occasionally experience the presence of the dead man's spirit in a variety of unexplained ways.

Hanging around to help food disappear as it emerges from the kitchen is probably one of the spirit's more vexing manifestations. I don't blame him, though, because the bountiful array of country-style food poses a definite temptation. Many of the recipes are from the Shenandoah Valley and have been handed down for generations.

I dined in a pre-Civil War room that was original to the house. I'm told that the room's beautiful pine walls were stripped of uncountable coats of paint during renovation. It was worth the effort as the wood adds a warm, rich feel to the room.

I enjoyed a tender and juicy London Broil for dinner with Mashed Potatoes, Broccoli Salad, Marinated Carrots and Spiced Fruits. That doesn't sound like typical country cooking, but it is of this region. I particularly liked the Broccoli Salad. I would also recommend the Fried Chicken or Oysters, and the Peanut Butter Pie was superb.

The Buckhorn stocks a good variety of domestic wines, particularly from the Shenandoah Vineyards. I didn't sample the wine as the atmosphere of the Buckhorn had already produced a mellowing effect that I didn't want to alter.

The Buckhorn Inn is located on Route 250 near Churchville. Meals are served Tuesday and Thursday from 11:00 a.m. until 9:00 p.m., and Wednesday and Friday from 11:00 a.m. until 4:00 p.m. Buffets are served on Wednesday, Friday and Saturday from 4:00 p.m. until 9:00 p.m., and Sunday from 11:00 a.m. until 8:00 p.m. No reservations are accepted. But if you need to call the inn for lodging, the phone number is (703) 885-2900.

BUCKHORN INN'S BROCCOLI SALAD

1 bunch broccoli, chopped	4 eggs, boiled and chopped
¼ cup onions, chopped	½ cup sugar
¼ cup green olives, chopped	1 cup mayonnaise

In a one-quart bowl, mix all ingredients together until mixture is well blended. Refrigerate. Serves 10 to 12.

BUCKHORN INN'S BAKED FRUIT

1½ cups sugar	2 cups chunk pineapple, drained
2 tablespoons cornstarch	
4 cups sliced peaches, drained	1 teaspoon ground cinnamon
4 cups sliced apples	½ teaspoon ground nutmeg
	¼ teaspoon curry powder

Mix together sugar and cornstarch and set aside. Combine fruits and sprinkle with cinnamon, nutmeg and curry. Add sugar mixture and stir well. Bake in 2½- to 3-quart ovenproof dish at 350 degrees for approximately 1 hour. Serves 10 to 12.

BUCKHORN INN'S MARINATED CARROTS

5 cups sliced carrots
1 medium onion
1 small green pepper
1 10½-ounce can of cream of
  tomato soup
½ cup salad oil
1 cup sugar

¾ cup cider vinegar
1 teaspoon prepared
  mustard
1 teaspoon Worcestershire
  sauce
1 teaspoon salt
½ teaspoon pepper

Put carrots in water and bring to a boil. Reduce heat to medium and cook until tender. Drain and cool. Cut onion and green pepper in round slices and mix with cooled carrots. Mix all other ingredients together in separate container and pour over vegetables. Cover and marinate in refrigerator for at least 12 hours. Drain to serve. Will keep for 2 weeks in refrigerator. Serves 8 to 10.

BUCKHORN INN'S PEANUT BUTTER PIE

⅓ cup creamy peanut butter
¾ cup confectioners' sugar

1 9-inch pie shell, baked

Mix peanut butter and sugar together until crumbly and place on bottom of crust, saving 2 tablespoons to sprinkle on top.

Filling:
⅓ cup flour
½ cup sugar
⅛ teaspoon salt
2 cups milk
2 egg yolks (slightly beaten)

2 teaspoons margarine,
  melted
1 teaspoon vanilla
prepared whipped topping

Mix first five ingredients together in a saucepan over high heat until mixture comes to a rolling boil. Stir until mixture reaches thick consistency. Remove filling from heat and add melted margarine and vanilla.

Pour over peanut butter mixture and cool. Spread with prepared whipped topping. Sprinkle with leftover peanut butter crumbles. Refrigerate. Yields 1 pie.

SKY CHALET COUNTRY INN
Basye

SKY CHALET
COUNTRY INN

Imagine a chalet nesting in the clouds: a haven so remote that the "frenzies" of this world are powerless to reach you. There is no television set or telephone in your room. You awaken to the aromas of fresh bread baking and coffee brewing. You slide from beneath comfy quilts and peer out of your window at the valley.

While your eyes feast on the surrounding Southern Alleghenies to the west or Massanutten Mountain to the east, the smell of that baking bread causes you to consider dressing for breakfast. There's no need to be fancy here; a pair of jeans and an old flannel shirt will be fine.

I ambled into the dining room on the cool spring morning to find a fire had already been started in the stone fireplace that reaches to the tip of the cathedral ceiling. Wanting a view of the mountains, I settled down at a table between two couples. One of my neighbors asked if I knew the time, and to my astonishment, I discovered that I had left my watch in the room. Both couples began to laugh with understanding. Forgetting to mark the passage of time is a fairly common occurrence in this relaxing setting.

In the midst of our amusement, the coffee arrived along with the baked bread, which was served in a clay flower pot. You could make a whole meal out of the Chalet's bread and jellies, but it's wise to leave room for their Potato Pancakes, fresh country Eggs, Sausage and gigantic Biscuits.

I had arrived late the night before, so I missed dinner. But my breakfast neighbors launched into full detail. It seems that their Barbecue, Rainbow Trout and Steak Teriyaki are all prepared in the traditional southern style. Dessert was one of their famous Shenandoah Fruit Cobblers.

Mention was also made of the good time had in the Supin Lick Pub, which serves some rather sophisticated cocktails and after-dinner drinks. I toured the rustic lounge, set up with backgammon and the only television set on the premises.

50

The Sky Chalet is where world-weary congressmen, famous newspeople and exhausted writers go into seclusion. You come here to eat well, sleep well and let the mountain air put your world back into perspective.

The Sky Chalet Country Inn is located ten miles from Mt. Jackson, off Route 263 West in Basye. Breakfast is served daily from 8:30 a.m. until noon; lunch is served from noon until 5:00 p.m. Dinner is served from 5:00 p.m. until 8:30 p.m. weekdays, and until 9:00 p.m. on weekends. For reservations (recommended on weekends) call (703) 856-2147.

SKY CHALET COUNTRY INN'S FLOWERPOT BREAD

1 package active dry yeast
¼ cup hot water
1 cup milk
4 cups all-purpose flour
½ stick margarine, room
  temperature

2 eggs
2 tablespoons sugar
½ tablespoon salt

In large mixing bowl place yeast and pour hot water over it to dissolve. In small saucepan scald milk and cool to lukewarm. Stir milk into yeast until combined. Sift flour and add with margarine, eggs, sugar and salt. Add to yeast mixture and beat until smooth. Place on floured board and knead for 4 to 5 minutes or until dough expands as if growing. Form into ball and place in a greased bowl, turning to coat dough on all sides. Cover and let rise in a warm place until it doubles (1½ to 2 hours). Punch dough down. Take a 6-inch clay gardening pot and line it with aluminum foil. Spray with nonstick cooking spray, and fill with dough. Return to warm place and let rise until doubled (about 1 hour). Bake in a preheated 425-degree oven for 25 to 30 minutes. Yields 1 loaf.

Note: A regular loaf pan can be used.

SKY CHALET COUNTRY INN'S APPLE COBBLER
WITH STREUSEL TOPPING

4 cups tart apples	1 cup light brown sugar
2 cups water	1 teaspoon lemon juice
½ teaspoon cinnamon	1 tablespoon cornstarch
¼ teaspoon nutmeg	

Peel, core and slice apples about ¼ inch thick. Place in a large pot with 2 cups water. Using medium low heat, cook about 3 minutes. Drain water, then add remaining ingredients. Reduce heat to low and cook until mixture slightly thickens. Set aside.

Batter:

1 cup flour	½ teaspoon salt
1 cup sugar	1 egg, beaten
1 teaspoon baking power	2 tablespoons butter, room temperature

Sift flour, sugar, baking powder and salt together in a bowl, and mix until thoroughly combined. Add egg, working into mixture. With two knives or pastry blender, cut butter into mixture until it reaches a pebbly consistency. With hands, knead gently into a ball. Flour board and roll out dough to fit a 7-inch by 12-inch baking pan. Grease pan and pour in apple mixture, distributing evenly. Fit rolled-out dough over top of mixture, seal the edges and prick with a fork in several places. Bake in a 350-degree oven for 30 minutes. Remove and distribute Streusel Topping evenly over cobbler. Return to oven and continue baking for an additional 30 minutes. Cool slightly and serve. Serves 8.

Streusel Topping:

1 stick butter	¾ cup plain flour
¼ cup light brown sugar	⅛ teaspoon lemon extract
¼ cup white sugar	

Cream butter and sugars together until coarse and crumbly. Add flour (all at once) and lemon extract to sugar and butter mixture. Mix until flour is moistened, but don't overbeat. Refrigerate briefly or until firm. Crumble topping evenly over apple cobbler.

McCORMICK'S PUB & RESTAURANT
Staunton

McCORMICK'S PUB & RESTAURANT

It is impossible to put a price on time, but when there is little, it becomes precious. Because Staunton's downtown business people have limited time for lunch, McCormick's has instituted what they call the Thirty-Minute Room. If you haven't been served and presented with your check within thirty minutes, your meal is free.

The Thirty-Minute Room's smart, green grasscloth walls and gold linen tablecloths do not suggest a "fast-food" affair; and indeed, you are not offered a "fast-food" menu.

The day I lunched in this tastefully decorated room, they were ready with an excellent Cabbage Soup containing garbanzo beans, chunks of sausage and bacon. This was *quickly* followed by a yummy Broccoli Cheddar Quiche with a hefty helping of authentic German Potato Salad and crisp Cole Slaw.

Dieters can always have a choice of slenderizing salads, but you might not want to diet, especially since that would mean giving up their famed Irish Whiskey Pie, which, thankfully, I did not. I didn't even go to their spa afterward to work off those extra calories, another option when dining at this restaurant.

McCormick's has access to a spa because it was originally a YMCA back in 1915. It seems that Staunton wanted a Y but could not come up with the necessary funds until someone got the idea to approach the Cyrus Hall McCormick family. The renowned farm machinery family offered to match whatever funds the city could raise. This innovative approach to philanthropy became the forerunner to the current method of matching grants.

At any rate, a sizable amount must have been raised as the interior is grand. You will be impressed with the handsome marble entrance leading to the former lobby, which now serves as a pub.

The lobby is paneled in walnut cut at the McCormick estate. This wood was used lavishly by skilled valley craftsmen to create everything from the mantle pieces to a wonderful, curving bar. Still ticking in the lobby after almost seven decades is a Seth Thomas clock, now valued at $10,000.

This luxuriously serene lobby is a great place to enjoy happy hour, particularly after a hectic day at work.

Dinner offers such gourmet specialties as the Fillet of Beef McCormick or the McCormick Reaper, which is roast beef and Brie on a croissant and accompanied by a stuffed potato.

Of course any of their luncheon or dinner meals may be complemented with a selection of imported wines and beers to afford you a pleasant experience at the old Y.

McCormick's is located at 41 North Augusta Street in Staunton. Lunch is served from 11:30 a.m. until 4:00 p.m.; dinner is from 5:30 p.m. until 9:30 p.m.; a pub menu is available from 4:00 p.m. until midnight, Monday through Saturday. On Sunday, brunch only is served from 11:30 a.m. until 3:00 p.m. For reservations (preferred) call (703) 885-3111.

McCORMICK'S IRISH WHISKEY PIE

1 tablespoon instant coffee
½ cup water
1 tablespoon gelatin
pinch of salt
¾ cup plus 2 teaspoons
  sugar

3 eggs, separated
6 tablespoons Irish whiskey
¼ cup Kahlúa
1 cup whipping cream
1 graham cracker crust,
  baked

Dissolve coffee in ¼ cup boiling water. Add enough cold water to make ½ a cup. In saucepan, mix coffee mixture, gelatin, salt, half of sugar and the egg yolks and heat slowly until slightly thickened but not congealed. Add whiskey and Kahlúa. Remove and let cool. Whip egg whites until stiff, not dry, adding remaining sugar very gradually. Gently fold egg whites into cooled coffee mixture. In separate bowl beat whipped cream until peaks form. Fold *gently* into coffee mixture. Spoon into prepared crust and chill at least 4 hours or until set. Yields 1 pie.

55

McCORMICK'S FILLET OF BEEF McCORMICK

2 to 3 tablespoons butter
1 shallot, chopped
6 ounces backfin crabmeat
½ teaspoon tarragon leaves
salt and pepper to taste
4 6- to 8-ounce filets
mignons, 1½ inches thick

Place butter in a large skillet and sauté shallots until soft. Add crabmeat, tarragon, salt and pepper and cook about 2 minutes to combine. Remove from skillet. Take a sharp knife and cut a pocket in each fillet and stuff with crab mixture. Return to skillet and cook on both sides until done. Top with Bearnaise Sauce (recipe below). Serves 4.

Bearnaise Sauce:
2 shallots, chopped
1 tablespoon tarragon
3 to 4 crushed white
    peppercorns
1 tablespoon parsley,
    chopped
1 bay leaf
pinch of thyme
2 ounces white wine
2 ounces cider vinegar
3 egg yolks
2 sticks butter, melted
juice of ½ a lemon

Place the shallots, tarragon, peppercorns, parsley, bay leaf, thyme, wine and vinegar in a saucepan and cook until liquid is reduced by a third. Beat egg yolks separately and add. Melt butter in separate pan and slowly pour into mixture. Add lemon juice. Place mixture in top half of double boiler and stir to thicken. Serve over fillets. Yields 1½ cups.

THE WHARF DELI & PUB
Staunton

THE WHARF DELI & PUB

I always thought the word "wharf" referred to the waterfront, so when there was no body of water anywhere near the Wharf Deli & Pub, I was confused. Then I discovered the Old English word "wharf" has another denotation. Wharf can also mean warehouse, which is what this restaurant, built as a grocery store in 1880, eventually became.

This interestingly mismatched brick building has passed from grocery store to veterinarian's hospital, and was last used as a garage and auto parts warehouse.

When the renovators began redesigning the building, they rescued a tremendous skylight from an old bank building slated for demolition. Installing the skylight into the second-floor roof opened the dark corners with a flood of sunlight and dramatically transformed the upstairs into a spacious room resembling an artist's loft. Large trees, planted in tubs, receive the necessary sunshine, and some leftover tin Coca Cola, Pepsi and Wolf's Head Oil signs are hung on the textured brick walls to strike a nostalgic chord from the past.

Sitting on an old wooden bench, I listened to the music drift upstairs. As a New York deli devotee, I was ecstatic to find the real thing in such pleasant surroundings, as delis are not known for especially attractive décor.

Whereas the house wine is usually a good barometer for formal restaurants, at a deli it's the chicken salad, slaw and potato salad that give the important clues. I check the usual meats and cheeses, but if a deli scores on their homemade items, then chances look good for the others. Verdict: The Chicken Salad was very good with nice chunks of chicken in a savory mixture, and the spicy, red cabbage Slaw was perfect with a light Coors beer. (You might want to try one of their other forty-nine imported beers.) Best of all was dessert. I took alternate bites of their German Chocolate Pie and Praline Eggnog Pie and never could decide which was the best, so I finished the last bite of each.

You'd think that dieting would be difficult, but they do offer a low-cal Cottage Cheese Plate with assorted cheeses for times when heavier selections are verboten.

The Wharf Deli & Pub is located at 123 South Augusta Street in Staunton. Food is served from 11:30 a.m. until 8:00 p.m., Monday through Thursday and from 11:30 a.m. until 9:30 p.m. on Friday and Saturday. The pub is open until 11:30 p.m. on Friday and until 1:00 a.m. on Saturday. For reservations (preferred for larger parties) call (703) 886-2329.

THE WHARF DELI'S CHICKEN SALAD

1 chicken, cooked and cut into bite-size pieces	1 teaspoon white pepper
1 medium onion, chopped	1 teaspoon salt
2 large celery stalks, chopped	1 teaspoon celery seeds
	¾ cup mayonnaise

After chicken has been cut into bite-size pieces, place in a bowl. Add chopped onion and chopped celery. Season with white pepper, salt and celery seeds. Spoon in mayonnaise and mix until all ingredients are thoroughly combined. Chill, covered in refrigerator. Serves 6 to 8.

THE WHARF DELI'S GERMAN CHOCOLATE PIE

4 ounces unsweetened chocolate	3 egg yolks
¼ cup butter	1 cup shredded coconut
1 cup sugar	1 unbaked pie shell
1 14-ounce can sweetened condensed milk	

Place chocolate and butter in a small saucepan over medium heat until melted, stirring constantly. Remove and pour chocolate mixture into bowl. Add sugar, beat with electric mixer. Stir in milk, mixing thoroughly. Add egg yolks, one at a time, beating until well incorporated. Add coconut. Pour chocolate mixture into pie shell and bake at 350 degrees for 45 to 50 minutes. Cool and serve. Yields 1 pie.

THE WHARF DELI'S PRALINE EGGNOG PIE

2 envelopes unflavored
  gelatin
¼ cup sugar
3 egg yolks
2 cups prepared eggnog
¼ cup praline extract or
  praline liqueur
1 teaspoon rum

½ teaspoon vanilla
1 cup heavy whipping
  cream
1 9-inch baked pie crust
ground nutmeg
whole cranberry sauce for
  garnish (optional)

In medium saucepan, mix gelatin with sugar. Blend in egg yolks that have been beaten with one cup of eggnog. Let stand one minute. Stir over low heat until gelatin is completely dissolved (about 5 minutes). Stir in remaining eggnog, praline extract or liqueur, rum and vanilla. Pour into large bowl and chill, stirring occasionally, until mixture mounds slightly when dropped from a spoon. Whip cream and fold gently into mixture. Turn into prepared crust; sprinkle with nutmeg. Chill until firm. Garnish with cranberry sauce if desired. Yields 1 pie.

THE BOAR'S HEAD INN
Charlottesville

THE BOAR'S HEAD INN

Eating dinner without a fork? Impossible, you say. It's possible and it happens each year at the Festival Before Forks, a sixteenth-century English banquet celebrated during Christmastime at the Boar's Head Inn. I'm told that some guests try to sneak in forks, but the strict rules require a humorous confiscation of the utensils.

Merrymaking abounds here under the "Lord of Misrule," where festivities include mumming (a Medieval word for dancing), wassailing, caroling and the performing of plays and music. This is definitely the place to enjoy Christmas if you're into fun and frolic, but there's something going on at this reconstructed 1834 gristmill any time of the year.

Their most famous dining room is the Old Mill Room, crowned with the original fourteen-inch thick, heart pine rough-hewn beams. This rustic room is softened with cornflower blue linen cloths and white carnations at each table. Beyond this dining area is a light and airy garden room overlooking a pond of mallards and visiting geese. My choice of dining, however, is outside beneath a gigantic sycamore, which is romantically lighted for evening diners.

Downstairs in the dining room, a band plays everything from old swing tunes to popular classics.

I sampled most of their entrées. The most unique to my palate was the Chicken Virginia, with the Lobster Tail vying for first place. I also enjoyed their preparation of Virginia Ham. The usual salty taste is ameliorated by the Raisin Sauce. The best Caesar Salad I've ever tasted is prepared tableside. Their research indicates that this unique salad is Mexican in origin, from Chef Caesar Cardini. This would be a nice dieter's choice, along with fresh broiled fish of the day. Dieters will probably have to whisper no to their heavenly desserts, especially the Satin Pie and Grand Marnier Cake.

The Boar's Head is particularly proud of their strong wine list, which offers a full variety of Virginia, California and imported selections.

If you visit in the warmer seasons you can go ballooning

on one of their champagne balloon flights. Sounds a bit heady for me; I'm much more inclined toward their hedonistic romp at Christmas.

The Boar's Head Inn is located three miles from Charlottes-ville on Highway 250 West. Breakfast is served Monday through Friday from 7:00 a.m. until 10:30 a.m., and lunch from noon until 2:00 p.m. Sunday brunch is served from 10:30 a.m. until 3:00 p.m. Dinner is served daily from 6:00 p.m. until 9:00 p.m. For reservations (required for dinner) call (804) 296-2181.

BOAR'S HEAD INN'S VIRGINIA HAM WITH RAISIN SAUCE

1 16- to 18-pound ham   **1 16-ounce can of peach halves**

Cover ham with water and soak overnight. Drain water and place ham in a large pot and cover with cold water. Bring to a simmer and cook for 2 to 3 hours, or until bone removes easily. Drain water and remove fat rind. Bake at 375 degrees for 45 minutes, glazing with juice from peaches. Garnish with peach halves and serve with Raisin Sauce (recipe below). Serves 12.

Raisin Sauce:

1 quart water   **1 cup cold water**
½ cup seedless raisins   **1 teaspoon salt**
2 oranges, juice only   **1 cup brown sugar**
1 lemon, juice only   **2 tablespoons cider vinegar**
4 tablespoons cornstarch

Fill a saucepan with 1 quart of water and add raisins. Simmer slowly until raisins are soft. Set aside. Combine orange and lemon juices and dissolve the cornstarch in this mixture with 1 cup of water. Add the cornstarch mixture to raisin mixture; cook, stirring with a wooden spoon, until thickened and glossy. Add salt, brown sugar and vinegar. Bring to a boil, remove from heat and serve with ham.

BOAR'S HEAD INN'S CHICKEN VIRGINIA

8 deboned chicken breasts
8 slices Virginia country
  ham

Sausage Stuffing (recipe
  below)
8 teaspoons butter

Flatten chicken breasts with mallet. Wrap one-eighth of the Sausage Stuffing with slice of ham. Fold the chicken breast around the ham and stuffing. Repeat for each serving. Place on greased pan, top each chicken breast with 1 teaspoon butter and bake at 350 degrees for 35 to 40 minutes. Top with Supreme Sauce (recipe below). Serves 8.

Sausage Stuffing:

½ cup sausage
½ cup onions, finely
  chopped
½ cup celery, finely
  chopped
4 cups bread crumbs

2 cups chicken stock or
  broth
4 eggs, beaten
2 tablespoons ground sage
black pepper and salt to
  taste

Cook sausage and crumble. Sauté onions and celery in sausage grease until soft. Drain grease. Mix the bread crumbs, chicken stock and eggs together and add the onions, celery, sausage, salt and pepper. Mix well.

Supreme Sauce:

2 tablespoons butter
2 tablespoons flour
2 cups clear chicken broth
2 tablespoons fresh
  mushrooms, chopped

1 small bay leaf
½ teaspoon salt
¼ teaspoon white pepper
⅛ cup heavy cream
2 egg yolks

In skillet, melt butter and stir in flour. Add chicken broth and stir until smooth. Add mushrooms, bay leaf, salt and pepper. Reduce heat, stirring occasionally for 30 minutes. Add cream and stir in yolks. Simmer 1 minute to heat through. Serve over chicken.

HOLLYMEAD INN
Charlottesville

HOLLYMEAD INN

If, after dining, you spend the night upstairs in the Blue Room, there's a chance that the ghost of a Hessian soldier will playfully snatch the pillow from beneath your sleeping head and toss it across the room.

Yes, in addition to haute cuisine, the Hollymead has a ghost. This spirit reportedly was a German soldier, one of many captured by General Horatio Gage in the 1777 Battle of Saratoga. The Hessians were marched to Virginia, where they were forced to build an additional penal facility to house themselves. That facility is now a part of the present structure of the Hollymead Inn. During the Hessians' imprisonment, one of the soldiers died, and his spirit seems to delight in playing pranks on the inn's caretakers.

I tried to talk my twenty-one-year-old daughter, Daintry, into sleeping in the Blue Room on the premise that spirits won't appear to me because they know I'll write about them. Her reply was a terse, "Bag it!" However, the next morning she did try to open a tiny closet in that room. The owners say the closet's door will open and close at will when the ghost is active, but can't be opened otherwise. She couldn't open the door but reported feeling a strange coldness surrounding the closet.

Daintry later told me she had considered snatching my pillow in the night, but decided against the prank, figuring I'd "freak out." Nor did she want to ruin our pleasant memories of the excellent time and meal we enjoyed at the inn.

Our meal took place the previous night on the garden porch. I had the succulent Bay Scallops with superb Carrots Cointreau, complemented by the dry, white house wine, Lion d'or Blanc de Blanc. Daintry selected the equally wonderful Veal with Chausseur Sauce. As both of us are chocoholics, we feasted on their Boule de Neige for dessert. Divine!

My meal was not exactly a low calorie one, but if that had been my intent I could have dined on their Grilled Chicken Teriyaki or Broiled Flounder and substituted the romantic atmosphere of this beautiful restaurant for dessert.

The Hollymead is located at 3001 Hollymead Drive, off Highway 29 North in Charlottesville. Lunch is served Tuesday through Friday from 11:30 a.m. until 1:00 p.m. Dinner is served Tuesday through Saturday from 5:30 p.m. until 10:00 p.m. Sunday brunch is served from 11:30 a.m. until 2:00 p.m. For reservations (recommended) call (804) 973-8488.

HOLLYMEAD INN'S BOULE DE NEIGE

16 ounces milk chocolate
2 individual serving
    packages or 2 teaspoons
    decaffeinated instant
    coffee
1 cup hot water

4 sticks sweet butter, room
    temperature
1 cup sugar
8 large eggs, beaten
½ cup creme de menthe

In top of double boiler, melt chocolate. Dissolve instant coffee in hot water and add to double boiler with one stick plus 2½ tablespoons of butter. Allow to melt and stir until mixed. Add sugar and stir; slowly pour half of chocolate into beaten eggs and stir to mix thoroughly. Pour egg and chocolate mixture back into double boiler and beat constantly with a heavy wire whisk. Remove pan from heat. Add remaining butter, beating to combine. Add creme de menthe and stir thoroughly. Double line a 2½-quart oven-proof ceramic or aluminum bowl with aluminum foil. Place mixture into bowl. Bake for 65 minutes or until thick crust forms on top. Cover and refrigerate for 3 days. Unmold from aluminum foil onto serving platter. If desired, decorate with stars of whipped cream using pastry tube. Serves 6 to 8.

HOLLYMEAD INN'S BAY SCALLOPS

Sauce:
1 cup white wine
2 shallots, finely chopped
1 teaspoon Pommery
    mustard grains

½ pint heavy cream
½ teaspoon arrowroot or
    cornstarch

In saucepan over high heat place wine, shallots and mustard grains and reduce liquid to half. Mix cream with arrowroot and add to saucepan; let boil to thicken slightly, stirring constantly. Reduce heat to simmer and stir occasionally.

1½ pounds bay scallops	1 teaspoon salt or to taste
2 cups white wine	½ teaspoon pepper or to taste

In separate saucepan, poach scallops in wine. Bring to boil, remove scallops, reduce liquid by half. Add sauce and reduce liquid by one-fourth to attain desired consistency. Salt and pepper to taste. Pour sauce over scallops. Serves 4.

HOLLYMEAD INN'S CARROTS COINTREAU

1½ pounds carrots	1 stick unsalted butter, melted
4 ounces Cointreau	1 teaspoon salt or to taste
¼ small can frozen orange juice concentrate or juice from 2 large oranges	½ teaspoon pepper

Peel and chop carrots into 2- to 3-inch chunks and boil in salted water until tender. Remove carrots and refresh in cold water. Drain. Using steel blade in food processor or blender, chop carrots fine. Place chopped carrots into a bowl and add Cointreau, orange juice concentrate and melted butter. Place mixture in a double boiler and reheat when ready to serve. Add salt and pepper to taste when hot. Serves 4 to 6.

THE IVY INN
Charlottesville

THE IVY INN

Uncle Sam is the real benefactor of higher prices. This is why The Ivy Inn's owner, Jean Abbott, prefers to pass the price savings on to her customers whenever possible. "After all," states Abbott, "I don't even know Uncle Sam!" That is why I found my special champagne to be priced a good five dollars less at this beguiling restaurant than I could find it elsewhere.

Built as a farmhouse in 1863, this appealing, red brick structure sits in front of the original five-cent toll turnpike. The house is surrounded with brightly colored flowers and looks as if it were someone's home. Once inside, you are treated as if you'd just dropped in for a meal at a friend's house.

Sitting in one of the downstairs dining rooms amidst a warm colonial décor, my daughter and I ordered their Champagne Melon Soup. What an appetizing way to begin a meal! Actually, the taste reminded me of a fancy champagne cocktail, with a somewhat stronger emphasis on fruit than wine.

Our appetizer was followed by a Spinach Salad with a most unusual warm and delicate dressing. Daintry tried the Chicken Pecan Waffle. This is a unique concoction of creamed chicken served over waffles and pecans, then garnished with spiced peaches and watermelon. I had to sample more than one bite of this scrumptious dish because one taste begged another.

We switched plates so Daintry could test my Scallop and Shrimp Casserole. We agree that this is a dish to please the taste buds of gourmet seafood lovers. Accompanying our lunch was a small loaf of freshly baked Sally Lunn Bread.

If trying to flatter your weight scale, you could enjoy either the Veal Supreme or their Steamed Lobster, Clams, Crab Legs and Shrimp served on a bed of greens.

Aside from its delicious cuisine, The Ivy Inn is also noted for its relaxing atmosphere. In fact, the atmosphere is so relaxing that an elderly couple takes naps between courses during their weekly dinner of salad, half an entrée each, half a carafe of wine and dessert.

70

Our dining experience was pleasantly concluded with hot Pecan Pie topped with whipped cream. The pie became a must for the recipe section. And on reflection, dining at The Ivy Inn is a must for anyone who appreciates good food in a congenial and unhurried atmosphere.

The Ivy Inn is located at 2244 Old Ivy Road in Charlottesville. Lunch is served from 11:30 a.m. until 2:00 p.m., Monday through Friday. Dinner is served from 5:00 p.m., Monday through Saturday. For reservations (recommended), call (804) 977-1222.

THE IVY INN'S PECAN PIE

3 eggs, beaten
1 cup dark corn syrup
½ cup sugar
½ teaspoon salt

1 teaspoon vanilla
1 cup pecan pieces or halves
1 8-inch unbaked pie shell

In bowl, combine all ingredients, except pecans, and beat well by hand until thoroughly combined. Place pecans in unbaked pie shell and pour liquid ingredients over top. Bake at 375 degrees for 45 minutes or until set. May serve with vanilla ice cream or whipped cream, if desired. Yields 1 pie.

THE IVY INN'S SCALLOP AND SHRIMP CASSEROLE

2 tablespoons butter
1 pound medium shrimp, cleaned
1 pound scallops
½ cup white wine
½ pound fresh mushrooms, sliced (or 1 small can of mushrooms)
1 10¾-ounce can cream of celery soup

1 cup sour cream
8 ounces sharp Cheddar cheese, grated
salt and pepper to taste
1 tablespoon Old Bay Seasoning
wild rice (follow package directions)

In skillet place butter and sauté shrimp and scallops until shrimp begin to turn pink and curl. Add wine, reduce heat to medium and cook for 2 minutes. Remove shrimp and scallops and set aside. Reduce heat to low; combine remaining ingredients, except rice, and add to skillet. Stir until well blended. Add shrimp and scallops and heat through. Serve over prepared wild rice. Serves 8 to 10.

THE IVY INN'S CHAMPAGNE MELON SOUP

⅛ of large watermelon, chopped
1 cantaloupe, chopped
juice of ½ lime
juice of ½ lemon
1 cup orange juice
1½ tablespoons honey
2 cups champagne

Chill bowls several hours before serving. Reserve a cup of watermelon and a cup of cantaloupe for garnish. Combine all ingredients, except champagne, and place in blender. Blend until puréed. Pour ¼ cup of champagne in each chilled bowl; add puréed mixture and top with watermelon and cantaloupe. Garnish with mint leaves or whipped cream, if desired. Serves 8.

LE SNAIL RESTAURANT
Charlottesville

**LE SNAIL
RESTAURANT**

If escargot is on the menu, you may be sure it will be my first choice, and dining at Le Snail, that seemed the most appropriate choice. The Austrian-trained chef and owner, Ferdinand Bazin, has given this appetizer a creative touch by nesting the escargot in puff pastry.

I began my sampling sitting on an old church pew in the bar, then moved into a beautiful back dining room where the walls had been painstakingly hand-stenciled by Bazin's wife, Judy. This type of stenciling, a French method too difficult to explain, creates an air of chic elegance.

Originally, Le Snail was a private residence. Built between 1880 and 1890, it later served as the home and office of the first black physician to graduate from the University of Virginia. That gentleman was Dr. Marshall T. Garrett, who did more for his community than minister to its ill health. In addition to his practice, Garrett became known as a community leader responsible for bringing about the reform of health care for prisoners.

It has been said that there are no accidents—fate directs our moves. Bazin believes Le Snail is housed in this quaint old home because of his own need for a physical examination. His first visit to the residence was as a patient, but his return was as master chef and proprietor.

Bazin puts special time and effort into creating his basically French cuisine. Another of my appetizer samplings was Smoked Salmon on freshly baked French bread with a dollop of Ravigot dressing. It was delicate and delicious, as was their Pâté made without preservatives. That evening I was having an appetizer feast, so I went on to sample their unique Bluefish. The fish is smoked and marinated to give it a distinct but delightful flavor.

Like most Americans, I grew up on *Peter Cottontail*, so it was difficult for me to even think of sampling the Lapin. But to my surprise, it was excellent! Bazin thinks rabbit will become the chicken of tomorrow. He could be right.

With my meal I sipped a most unusual white house wine

called Papillon de la Reine. This translates as "Butterfly of the Queen," a whimsical name for a superior house wine.

I bowed out of dessert but would recommend the Crepe Maison flambéed tableside. It looked most appealing.

The Bazins were labeled "brave pioneers" when they restored their restaurant, and their courage and artistry have created a success.

Le Snail is located at 320 West Main Street in Charlottesville. Dinner is served Monday through Saturday from 6:00 p.m. until 10:00 p.m. The restaurant is closed for three weeks in both August and December. For reservations (recommended) call (804) 295-4456.

LE SNAIL'S CRAB AU FOUR

1 pound crabmeat, drained
1 tablespoon salt
½ tablespoon pepper
½ tablespoon chopped
   garlic clove
2 tablespoons
   Worcestershire sauce
1 lemon rind, grated
3 teaspoons parsley,
   chopped
¼ cup white wine

½ cup sliced mushrooms
2 tablespoons hazelnuts,
   chopped
½ cup onions, chopped
1 cup sour cream
juice of 1 lemon
¼ cup bread crumbs, fine
Hollandaise sauce (use
   prepared mix or your
   favorite recipe)
optional garnish

Combine all ingredients except Hollandaise in bowl and mix thoroughly. Let set for thirty minutes. Spoon into 12 individual oven-proof dishes or large casserole dish. Cover with Hollandaise and bake at 350 degrees for 15 minutes. Garnish with lemon slices, tomatoes, cucumbers and sprigs of parsley if desired. Serves 12 appetizers or 6 entrées.

LE SNAIL'S FILLET LAPIN

2 2- to 3-pound rabbits or
   fillets
4 slices bacon
pinch of salt, pepper,
   paprika and thyme

flour to dust
1 tablespoon oil
1 apple, sliced
prepared rice
grapes (optional)

Preheat oven to 425 degrees. Wrap rabbit tenderloins (or boned rabbits) with bacon strips and secure with toothpicks. Season with salt, pepper, paprika and thyme. Roll in flour and shake off excess. Put oil in hot oven-proof skillet and sear rabbits on all sides. Place in oven with apple slices on top for 10 minutes or until fully cooked. Arrange rabbit on platter with rice. Top with sauce (recipe below) and garnish with baked apple slices and grapes. Serves 6 to 8.

Sauce:

1 stick butter
2 onions, chopped
¾ pound mushrooms
3 tablespoons parsley
1 tablespoon garlic,
   chopped
⅛ teaspoon thyme
⅛ teaspoon rosemary
1 bay leaf

6 juniper berries
1 cup ginger-flavored
   currant wine
2 teaspoons salt
1 teaspoon white pepper
½ cup sour cream
½ cup half and half
2 tablespoons flour

In skillet, melt butter and sauté onions. Add mushrooms, parsley, garlic, thyme, rosemary, bay leaf and juniper berries and cook for 1 minute. Add wine, salt and pepper; bring to boil. Reduce and simmer for 5 minutes. Meanwhile, combine sour cream, half and half and flour. Whisk until smooth. Stir into sauce and simmer for 5 minutes. Serve with rabbit. Also good with chicken and veal. Serves 8.

MICHIE TAVERN
Charlottesville

MICHIE TAVERN

Michie Tavern may have been America's first drive-in bar. Back in 1746, "Scotch" John Michie, exiled from Scotland for his religious beliefs, opened the doors of his ordinary and tavern to weary travelers. The "gentlemen" travelers could partake of spirits produced by E.C. Booze (hence the origin of liquor's slang term) inside the tavern's Tap Room. However, their stagecoach drivers could only be served from the outside bar on the front porch.

The outside bar is still there and the tavern appears today much as it did to our early ancestors, except apple cider instead of "booze" is served in tin cups.

Guests proceed through the log and clay-plastered dining room to a cafeteria arrangement. There your tin plate may be filled with as much as you please of Fried Chicken, Potato Salad, Green Beans, Black-Eyed Peas, Corn Bread, Biscuits, Fruit Cobbler and the best Stewed Tomatoes in Virginia.

All the recipes are faithfully reproduced from colonial days, even the Stewed Tomatoes, which were called the devil's apple back then. This "apple" was thought to induce passion and was therefore forbidden. So, try this recipe at your own discretion.

Michie and his wife, Mary, expanded their facilities to include a general store and a gristmill. A few years ago, the whole operation was disassembled, numbered and moved eighteen miles to its current mountain-top site. This location is perfect, as it commands a breathtaking view of Charlottesville.

Either before or after dining, you may browse through the general store. The store's counter and display cases were purchased from Ike Godsey, the real storekeeper characterized on the TV program *The Waltons*.

When visiting Michie Tavern, do allow enough time to see their museum. It will give you an authentic taste of how our ancestors prepared meals, entertained and slept at an ordinary. A copy of their rules stipulated: "Only five to a bed; no

boots worn in bed; no tinkers or monkey grinders allowed."
I certainly concur with the "no boots" rule.

More seriously, though, I am especially pleased to report that the tavern complex is currently rehabilitating several old buildings where handicapped workers will produce their crafts. This project is exactly in keeping with the spirit of John Michie, who saw America as a nation of understanding and tolerance.

Michie Tavern is located on Route 53 near Monticello. Lunch is served daily from 11:15 a.m. until 3:30 p.m. in the summer and from 11:30 a.m. until 3:00 p.m. other seasons. The Spring House is open for light meals from 9:00 a.m. until 4:30 p.m. in June, July and August. Reservations are not accepted except for parties of 15 or more. The phone number is (804) 977-1234.

MICHIE TAVERN'S STEWED TOMATOES

4 cups whole tomatoes,
   peeled and quartered
½ cup sugar
¼ stick butter, melted
½ teaspoon salt
6 baked Biscuits,
   (recipe below)

In a saucepan, combine tomatoes, sugar, butter and salt. Crumble biscuits over the mixture. Cover and cook over a medium heat for 15 minutes. Serves 6.

MICHIE TAVERN'S BISCUITS

2 cups all-purpose flour
2 teaspoons baking powder
¼ teaspoon salt
3 tablespoons shortening
⅔ cup milk

Sift together flour, baking powder and salt. Add shortening and stir in milk quickly with fork, making dough light and fluffy but not sticky. Take dough and knead by hand until it is smooth, approximately 20 times. Roll out dough on lightly floured board to ½-inch thickness. Cut into biscuits. Bake on greased cookie sheet at 450 degrees for 12 to 16 minutes. Yields 14 to 16 biscuits.

MICHIE TAVERN'S COLONIAL FRIED CHICKEN

¾ cup all-purpose flour
1½ tablespoons oregano
½ teaspoon paprika
1 teaspoon garlic salt
¼ teaspoon pepper
1 2- to 3-pound fryer, cut up
3 cups shortening

Combine flour with oregano, paprika, garlic salt and pepper. Roll the chicken, piece by piece, in the mixture until well-coated. Melt shortening in heavy, cast-iron skillet or Dutch oven to 350 degrees. Fry chicken for 12 to 15 minutes on each side, or until tender. Serves 4 to 6.

MICHIE TAVERN'S APPLE COBBLER

¾ cup sugar
2 tablespoons flour, if fruit
 is juicy
⅛ teaspoon salt
½ teaspoon grated lemon
 peel
1½ teaspoons lemon juice
1 teaspoon nutmeg
½ teaspoon cinnamon
6 to 7 cooking apples,
 peeled, cored and thinly
 sliced
Pie Crust (see Index)
1 tablespoon butter

In a mixing bowl combine all ingredients except apples, pie crust and butter. Prepare pie crust and line either large oven-proof square or rectangular dish; add half of apples and sprinkle with half of sugar mixture. Top with remaining apples and remaining sugar mixture. Dot with butter. Add top crust, rolled to desired thickness. Make slits for steam to escape, and dot with more butter. Place pie in a 450-degree, pre-heated oven and bake for 40 to 50 minutes. Serves 15.

MILLER'S
Charlottesville

MILLER'S

As a child I could hold on to money only until I got to the store—the drugstore, that is. There, my nickel was traded for a Cherry Coke mixed to order at the soda fountain.

The day I walked into Miller's, a drugstore from 1880 until 1975, those memories came flooding back. The high, sculptured-tin ceiling, old mosaic tile floors and walls lined with rich cherry and mahogany shelves were part of my past. The soda fountain, now a bar, still retains the handsome old mirror installed by the original owner, Dr. G.T. Miller.

The current owner showed me one of Dr. Miller's own patent medicines that had made the doctor well known in Charlottesville. The medication was called "Egyptian Herb Tonic for Women." The label read, "This prescription is the favorite prescription of a Practicing Physician and is especially useful in those disorders of the system peculiar to women."

I don't wonder—the tonic contained twelve percent alcohol! The label's explanation went on: "Remember its field of usefulness begins with early adolescence and continues clear through life and old age." Does that mean old age is a stage after life? I wonder, but apparently it didn't confuse Dr. Miller's patients, or after drinking several bottles they ceased to care.

I do know that I was happy to have found this old drugstore, even if I couldn't get a Cherry Coke. Instead, I had an Italian pastry called Calzone. Naturally, I wanted the recipe for this hearty meal. It didn't remind me of Italian cooking, but it was very good, nonetheless.

I went on to sample their delicious Jambalaya, reminiscent of New Orleans, served with hot, freshly baked muffins. I finished with a serving of their heavenly Chocolate Mousse.

My meal was accompanied by music that sounded as if it came from an old player piano, but I'm told that dinner guests are treated to live jazz and blues on the weekends. Guests also have the option of outside dining, where alcoholic beverages can be served only during evening hours.

The dinner menu becomes more sophisticated, offering such dishes as Beef Bourguignon and Broiled Fish.

For those who want something different from the usual fare, nostalgic Miller's is your kind of place.

Miller's is located at 109 West Main Street in Charlottesville. Lunch is served from 11:30 a.m. until 2:00 p.m., Monday through Friday; dinner is from 6:00 p.m. until 9:30 p.m., Monday through Saturday. For reservations (recommended) call (804) 971-8511.

MILLER'S JAMBALAYA

2 tablespoons butter
4 slices bacon, chopped
1 large onion, chopped
1 bay leaf
½ teaspoon thyme
2 16-ounce cans peeled
 tomatoes
3 cloves garlic, chopped
¼ green bell pepper,
 chopped

1 tablespoon Worcestershire
 sauce
dash of Tabasco sauce
¼ teaspoon cayenne
salt and pepper to taste
3 cups rice (follow package
 directions)
2 cups chicken, cooked
1 pound medium shrimp,
 cleaned

Melt butter in large Dutch oven and sauté bacon, onions, bay leaf and thyme. Lower heat and add tomatoes and cook 5 minutes. Add garlic, green pepper, Worcestershire sauce, Tabasco sauce, cayenne, salt and pepper. Cook for 30 minutes, stirring frequently. Meanwhile, prepare rice in separate saucepan. Stir in chicken and cook for 5 minutes. About 7 minutes before serving, stir in rice and shrimp. Serves 8.

MILLER'S CHOCOLATE MOUSSE

3 eggs, separated
4½ ounces chocolate chips

1¼ cups whipped cream
1 tablespoon creme de cacao

Separate yolks from whites of eggs (reserving whites) and set aside. Melt chocolate in saucepan over low heat, add yolks. Stir until well blended; cool. Whip cream and fold in cooled chocolate/egg mixture with creme de cacao. In separate bowl, beat egg whites until stiff and gently fold into chocolate cream mixture. Pour into 8 individual molds or one 2½-quart mold. Chill until set. May garnish with additional whipped cream if desired. Serves 8.

MILLER'S CALZONE

Pastry:

3 cups all-purpose flour	⅓ cup margarine
1 cup whole wheat flour	⅓ cup shortening
1¼ tablespoons salt	buttermilk as needed

In mixing bowl, measure flour and salt together. Quarter margarine and shortening into cubes and add to bowl. Work the dough by hand, adding buttermilk a tablespoon at a time until kneaded to a pliable dough consistency. Cover and refrigerate.

Filling:

1½ cups Ricotta cheese	¼ teaspoon thyme
¼ cup Parmesan cheese	1 egg, beaten
salt and pepper to taste	1 cup ham, diced

In mixing bowl, combine all ingredients. Take dough and divide it into 6 equal balls. On floured surface, roll out dough to ¼-inch thickness. Place ⅙ of filling mixture on dough and fold dough in half, forming a half-moon shape. Pinch edges together and prick dough with a fork. Repeat until all are filled. Place on greased baking sheet and bake in a 350-degree oven approximately 20 minutes. Serves 6.

THE VIRGINIAN
Charlottesville

THE VIRGINIAN During the depression, people found that it was important to indulge the human spirit in small but special ways. One very nourishing way, for both soul and body, was an occasional visit to Charlottesville's oldest downtown restaurant, The Virginian.

Established in 1921 across from the University of Virginia, this quaint college hangout of yesteryear was often mentioned on the popular TV program, *The Waltons*. How often John Boy actually visited the restaurant is unknown, but the fact that it was a popular retreat, even in depression years, attests to its fine food and casual atmosphere.

Today, old-fashioned fans hang from a white-latticed ceiling that sets off the dark wood halls and private booths.

I was quite surprised to discover that the menu did not reflect what I would have expected to be typical fare for college students, but then I also learned that while the restaurant is frequented by a youngish clientele, only about a third of them are students.

A spicy yet hearty bean soup called Caldo Gallego was a marvelous way to tease my taste buds, along with a wonderful light luncheon entrée (or appetizer) made with shrimp, tomatoes, Feta cheese and fresh basil. I washed it all down with a red Bordeaux wine.

If you are in the mood for something lighter than their luncheon burgers and Mexican dishes, you could have a special vegetarian dish for either lunch or dinner.

The dessert that seemed just the right accompaniment for my spicy meal was their Almond Custard, but don't think I didn't have a go at their Chocolate Pecan Pie. It's a fat day indeed when I pass up chocolate.

When visiting for an evening meal you might want to try one of their special fish or chicken dinners, along with an inventive cocktail dreamed up at the bar.

On a lazy weekend, think of stopping by for brunch and investigate their Eggs Chesapeake. This dish is sautéed crabmeat and tomatoes served on an English muffin and topped with a poached egg and Hollandaise sauce.

The Virginian is a restaurant that doesn't rely on old stand-bys, but prefers to create and experiment with new dishes on a daily basis. And that plays a big part in the fun of going there.

The Virginian is located at 1521 West Main Street in Charlottesville. Meals are served from 9:00 a.m. until 11:00 p.m. daily, with the exceptions of Saturday and Sunday when brunch is served from 10:00 a.m. until 3:00 p.m. Reservations are not accepted, but the phone number is (804) 293-2606.

THE VIRGINIAN'S CHOCOLATE PECAN PIE

¼ pound or 1 stick melted butter
1¼ cups brown sugar
1¼ cups light corn syrup
5 eggs
1½ teaspoons vanilla
1 tablespoon rum
1 9-inch pie shell
¾ cup chocolate chips
1 cup pecan halves

Cream butter and brown sugar thoroughly with electric mixer; gradually add corn syrup. Beat in eggs, one at a time. Add vanilla and rum. Sprinkle pie shell with chocolate chips and pecans. Pour in filling. Bake at 350 degrees until set, about 40 to 50 minutes. Yields 1 pie.

THE VIRGINIAN'S FETA, BASIL, SHRIMP & TOMATO PASTA SAUCE

1 pound tiny shrimp, cleaned
juice of ½ a lemon
water to cover shrimp
4 tomatoes, peeled, cored and chopped
10 fresh basil leaves, chopped
½ medium onion, chopped
¾ cup olive oil
5 ounces Feta cheese
linguine or fettucine noodles (follow package directions)

Poach shrimp in saucepan with lemon and water about 1 to 2 minutes. Remove, drain and cool. In separate container, combine tomatoes, basil leaves, onion and olive oil and stir thoroughly. Add cooled shrimp and Feta cheese. Serve over linguine or fettucine noodles. Serves 6 to 8.

THE VIRGINIAN'S CALDO GALLEGO
(BEAN SOUP)

1 pound pinto beans
2 quarts water
8 strips bacon
1 pound bulk sausage
1½ medium onions, thinly
   sliced
5 garlic cloves, chopped
1 16-ounce can whole
   peeled tomatoes
1 can chicken broth or stock

3 carrots, thinly sliced
3 potatoes, peeled and
   thinly sliced
1 teaspoon pepper
1 teaspoon salt or to taste
2 bay leaves
1 10-ounce package frozen
   spinach
¼ cup white wine

Soak beans overnight in water in large soup kettle. The next day bring water to boil and reduce heat to simmer. Cook until beans are tender, about 6 to 8 hours. Meanwhile, cook bacon; set aside and reserve bacon drippings. In separate pan, sauté sausage by crumbling as it is added to pan and turning until done but not browned. Drain sausage. Sauté onions and garlic in bacon drippings. Drain. When beans are tender, add all other ingredients except spinach and wine. Simmer until potatoes and carrots are tender, about an hour. During the last 15 minutes, add spinach and wine. More chicken broth may be added for a thinner soup. Serves 12 generously.

PROSPECT HILL
Trevilians

PROSPECT HILL

Author Margaret Mitchell could have been writing about Prospect Hill in *Gone With The Wind*. The spring morning that I drove past the boxwood hedge I glimpsed the Manor House through the English tree garden, wreathed in a pastel coiffure of blossoming dogwoods. The 1732 house, now surrounded by renovated slave quarters, was originally converted from a barn when the Roger Thompson family's log cabin burned. The following year, Richmond Terrill took over the property and began shaping it into a plantation. When William Overton purchased it in 1840, two additional wings and a spiral staircase were added to the frame home.

After the Civil War, Prospect Hill faced a dilemma that was common among plantations. Fortunately, the house was not burned, but the plantation had to function without labor or capital. For sixteen years the Overtons eked out a subsistance, then finally, taking the cue from other plantations, opened their home to guests. Thus, for over one hundred years this home has maintained the integrity of genteel hospitality that the South seems to have patented. True Southern hospitality is endangered these days and too often supplanted with phony substitutions.

"Prospect Hill is small," explains owner, Bill Sheehan, and its very smallness helps him and his wife Mireille combat the mediocrity they have experienced in too many other so-called "Southern" settings.

It is Mireille's French heritage that is aromatically detected from the kitchen, where the primary focus is on preparing fresh food naturally.

Overnight guests can either have breakfast in bed or dine in the blue and white colonial breakfast room, after Bill clangs the bell. The meal is always a surprise. That morning freshly squeezed orange juice arrived in a wine glass, followed by fried Apple Fritter Pancakes and coffee. Guests from distant states joined me in appreciation of this perfectly executed meal. They also offered satisfied remarks about their previous night's dinner of Onion Soup, Salad Vinaigrette and continental-style Roast Beef served with Red Potatoes and Asparagus, ending with a Strawberry Cream Torte.

Each evening at the set-priced meal, guests may purchase either a Virginia or French wine to enhance the meal.

The restaurant operates in a mode similar to that of a family. Meals are designed by the family head and substitutions (say, for dieters) are accommodated. They won't force you to eat something you hate, as your mother did, but choices are limited. This has never been a deterrent, as guests enjoy the element of surprise which comes not only from the menu but also from the entertainment. Depending on the season, you may be entertained by a classical guitar, dulcimer or a storyteller who spins yarns out on the wicker bedecked porch before the dinner bell clangs.

Chefs in the region told me that they chose to dine at Prospect Hill on their nights off. What better compliment can be paid?

Prospect Hill is located near Zion Crossroads on Route 613 in Trevilians. Dinner is served Wednesday and Thursday at 7:30 p.m., and at 8:00 p.m. on Friday and Saturday. Breakfast is served to lodging guests only. For reservations (required) call (703) 967-0844.

PROSPECT HILL'S FRITTATA ZUCCHINI

1 pound zucchini or yellow squash

6 eggs
½ cup Mozzarella cheese

Peel zucchini and shred, using largest hole in grater or food processor. Grease a 12-inch by 16-inch oven-proof dish or casserole and place shredded zucchini on bottom. Beat eggs and pour over zucchini. Sprinkle shredded cheese over top and bake in top third of 350-degree oven until lightly browned, about 30 to 40 minutes. Serves 4 to 6.

PROSPECT HILL'S APPLE FRITTER PANCAKES

Pancake Batter:

3 eggs	1 teaspoon baking soda
⅔ cup all-purpose flour	1 teaspoon baking powder
1 cup milk	2 tablespoons vegetable oil
1 tablespoon sugar	

In blender or with electric beater, combine all ingredients except oil and blend until smooth. (Let set 10 to 15 minutes for a thin batter.)

Add oil to skillet and swirl to coat bottom over medium-high heat. Pour or ladle batter into desired size of pancake (1½ to 3 tablespoons) and cook until edges are lightly browned. Turn pancake to cook other side. Repeat until all batter is used, stacking pancakes on a dish. Keep warm in 150-degree oven.

12 slices bacon	1 teaspoon lemon juice or
2 to 3 medium-sized apples	vinegar
2 tablespoons butter	

Fry bacon in large cast-iron skillet and set bacon aside. Drain skillet and reserve drippings. Peel and slice apples ¼-inch thick and chop coarsely. Place in bowl of cold water with lemon juice or vinegar and set aside for 5 to 10 minutes. Drain apples, drying them with a paper towel. Add about 2 tablespoons of the bacon drippings and the butter to a clean skillet and heat over medium-high heat, swirling drippings and butter until well combined. Sauté apples for 2 to 3 minutes until lightly browned, being careful not to overcook. Remove from pan. Place 2 or more tablespoons of cooked apples on each pancake and roll up and keep warm in oven until ready to serve. Serve with bacon. Yields 12 to 16 pancakes, depending on size.

BAVARIAN CHEF
Madison

BAVARIAN CHEF

A soup to cure sinus? You've got to be kidding. But a sampling of Hungarian Goulash Soup created by Chef Jerome Thalwitz made a believer out of me.

I stumbled upon this medical discovery quite by accident. My Virginia friends had told me about this restaurant, described by *The New York Times* as offering "one of the best German meals available anywhere." Therefore, on my last trip to Virginia, I scheduled a detour.

Upon arrival, my daughter Daintry was suffering with sinus problems. When Thalwitz realized her discomfort, a special soup was suggested to alleviate her condition. When the steaming bowl arrived, Daintry's wan smile wore an edge of uncertainty, but politely, she began to sample. After a couple of spoonfuls, she interrupted my conversation with Thalwitz demanding, "Mother, get this recipe!" She was so insistent that another bowl of their delicious, magical potion was brought for me.

My friends did not know about this soup when they recommended the restaurant. They had raved about the Mandelschnitzel, which I discovered is pork baked in a wonderful strawberry and gin sauce. The unusual combination makes the dish superb.

If doing a calorie cheat, try their Filet Mignon or Zwiebelbraten, a roast beef cooked in beer and onions.

They offer a wine list that is neither extravagant nor pretentious, but skillfully designed to complement the food. Actually, there is not an ounce of pretense in this Bavarian-American restaurant.

The upstairs has the appearance of an old Bavarian inn, with its wood beams and German décor, while the downstairs features a large mural of Southern Bavaria. It was while sitting opposite this rendering of a famous Bavarian castle that we concluded our meal with a Grand Marnier Creme Torte that could provoke hazardous driving. For authentic Bavarian food with a creative touch, try this old converted truck stop. Some truck stop!

The Bavarian Chef is located on Highway 29, about 5 miles south of Madison. Dinner is served Tuesday through Saturday from 4:30 p.m. until 10:00 p.m. Meals are served from 11:30 a.m. until 10:00 p.m. on Sunday. For reservations (required) call (703) 948-6505.

BAVARIAN CHEF'S GRAND MARNIER CREME TORTE

12 ounces sweet chocolate	1 ounce brandy
2 sticks margarine	1 ounce light rum
½ cup cocoa	graham cracker crust in
½ cup sugar	9-inch pan, baked

In a saucepan over medium heat, melt chocolate and margarine. Stir in cocoa and sugar. When combined, add brandy and rum and mix thoroughly. Pour mixture into graham cracker crust and freeze.

Cream Filling:

6 egg yolks	½ cup Grand Marnier (or to
⅓ cup sugar	taste)
1 cup whipping cream	

With electric mixer, combine egg yolks and sugar and beat until mixture doubles. Put in refrigerator until chilled. Whip cream and slowly fold cream into sugar mixture. Slowly add Grand Marnier. Pour on top of first layer and freeze. Cover with plastic wrap. Yields one torte.

BAVARIAN CHEF'S MANDELSCHNITZEL

2 eggs	4 6-ounce pork tenderloins
2 cups fine bread crumbs	flour for dredging
2 ounces blanched almonds, sliced	3 tablespoons butter

Beat eggs. In separate bowl, combine bread crumbs and almonds. Lightly dredge pork in flour. Dip in egg batter, and roll in bread crumb mixture to cover. Melt 3 tablespoons butter in large skillet and sauté pork until golden brown on both sides. Remove from pan, place on platter and keep warm. Serves 4.

Sauce:

2 tablespoons butter	1 ounce kirschwasser (or
1 small onion, chopped	kirsch)
1 cup chicken stock or broth	¼ cup cornstarch
5 ounces strawberry	¾ cup water
preserves	cayenne to taste
2 tablespoons sugar	1 lemon, sliced
1 ounce gin	

Melt 2 tablespoons butter in skillet and sauté onions until soft. Add chicken stock, strawberry preserves, sugar, gin and kirschwasser. Mix cornstarch and ¾ cup water in cup and stir until cornstarch is dissolved. Add to sauce and stir thickened. Sprinkle with cayenne to taste. Place sauce on warmed plates and lay pork on top. Garnish with lemon slices. Serves 4.

BAVARIAN CHEF'S HUNGARIAN GOULASH SOUP

4 sticks margarine	3 tablespoons Hungarian
1 pound top round steak,	paprika (no substitutes)
cut into bite-size pieces	2 bay leaves
2 large onions, chopped	2 cups beef stock
¼ cup ground beef	white pepper and salt to
2 lemon peels, finely grated	taste
2 tablespoons caraway seeds	cayenne to taste
1 tablespoon garlic salt	2 tablespoons flour
	½ cup water

In heavy Dutch oven, melt margarine as needed and sauté steak, onions and ground beef. Reduce heat and add lemon peels, caraway seeds, garlic salt, Hungarian paprika, bay leaves and beef stock. Simmer over medium heat for at least 1 hour. Add salt, white pepper and cayenne to taste. Mix flour in half a cup of water and add to mixture. Stir until soup thickens slightly. Serves 10 to 12.

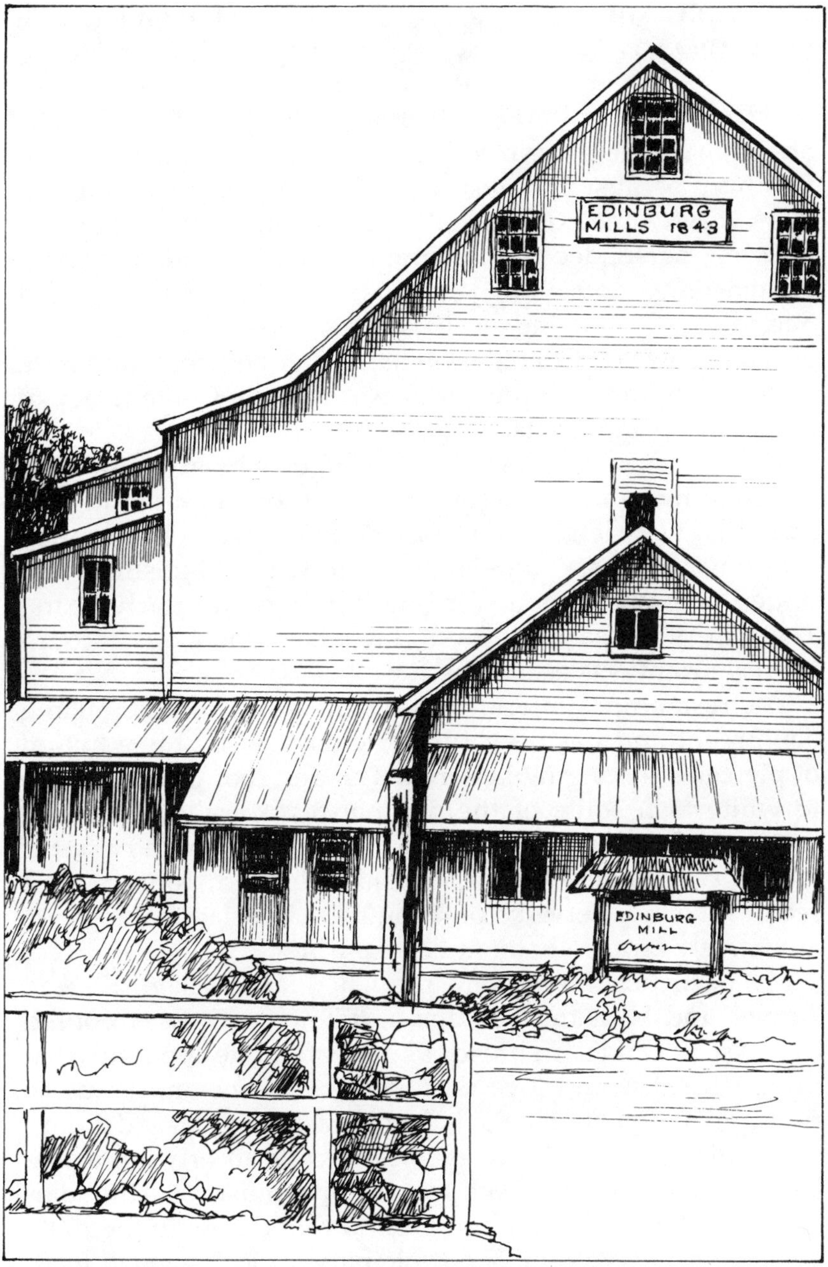

EDINBURG MILL RESTAURANT

Edinburg

EDINBURG MILL RESTAURANT

Would one of today's female teen-agers risk her life for what she believes?

During the Civil War, a teen-ager did just that. General Sheridan's raiders twice set fire to the 1848 Grandstaff Mill in Edinburg because it was supplying flour to Confederate soldiers. Each time, Grandstaff's granddaughters, Nellie and Melvina, persuaded the General to order his soldiers to help townswomen douse the flames. Afterwards, Nellie charmed Sheridan into allowing her to ride his horse. The resourceful girl then sewed a Confederate flag to her petticoats and rode audaciously through the valley warning the Confederacy of Sheridan's plan for attack.

The mill survived, and the charred embers at the front of the building continue to serve as a footnote representing the scars that were left by America's darkest page in history.

Survival is what counts, though, and this old gristmill continued to produce flour for one hundred and thirty years. Then, in 1978, the gears ground to a halt, and a classy country restaurant was established.

The restaurant's interior has retained much of the milling equipment and has been further enhanced by the addition of pierced-tin hanging lanterns. The designer cleverly chose to whitewash some of the original plank walls and adorn them with Edinburg memorabilia. The achieved country-casual look is coordinated with good old-fashioned, country-style recipes. Food is served from a buffet, and salad makings are attractively arrayed in an antique purifier.

My particular loves were the Cheddar Chicken, Stewed Apples and both the Sausage and Tomato Gravies poured over biscuits and corn bread. I knew, after one spoonful, that my husband would love that Sausage Gravy, and I was so right. Their Toll House Pie is an old-fashioned taste delight.

You also can imbibe your favorite cocktail or wine in the Lazy Miller Lounge, which features live music on Thursday, Friday and Saturday nights. I found that dining in the mill's casual atmosphere provided triple pluses: old fashioned food, relaxation and reminders of our resourceful past.

The Edinburg Mill Restaurant is located on Route 11 on the south edge of town. Meals are served daily. Breakfast is served from 7:00 a.m. until 11:00 a.m. The luncheon buffet is served from 11:00 a.m. until 2:00 p.m., but sandwiches are available all day. Dinner is from 5:00 p.m. until 10:00 p.m. For reservations (required) call (703) 984-8555.

EDINBURG MILL RESTAURANT'S SAUSAGE GRAVY

1 pound mild sausage
4 tablespoons onion, finely
  chopped
2 tablespoons sugar
1 teaspoon salt
½ teaspoon pepper

2 tablespoons
  Worcestershire sauce
¼ cup plain flour
½ cup water
½ cup milk
dash of Kitchen Bouquet

Brown sausage in a skillet, adding one tablespoon at a time to prevent sticking. When sausage is browned, add onions, sugar, salt, pepper and Worcestershire sauce and simmer for two minutes. Add flour, sprinkling evenly on top of sausage. Add water and milk gradually until the right consistency is achieved. Add a dash of Kitchen Bouquet for color. Simmer for 10 to 15 minutes. Serves 6 to 8.

EDINBURG MILL RESTAURANT'S TOMATO GRAVY

4 tablespoons butter
4 tablespoons onion, finely
  chopped
½ cup flour
2 cups canned tomatoes,
  chopped and including
  juice

1 teaspoon salt, or to taste
½ teaspoon pepper
2 tablespoons sugar
dash of Worcestershire
  sauce
dash of celery salt

Melt butter in skillet and add onions. Sauté until transparent. Reduce heat and gradually add flour, stirring to prevent lumping. Cook until brown, and add tomatoes (including juice). Blend tomatoes into mixture. Add salt, pepper, sugar, Worcestershire sauce and celery salt. Simmer 10 to 15 minutes and serve over hot homemade biscuits. Serves 6 to 8.

EDINBURG MILL RESTAURANT'S
CHEDDAR CHICKEN

1 package Cheddar Cheese
Goldfish crackers

1 stick melted butter
4 chicken breasts

Coat baking sheet with non-stick cooking spray. Crush crackers in blender and set aside. Melt butter in saucepan. Dip chicken in melted butter and dredge in crushed crackers. Place on baking sheet and bake in 350-degree oven for one hour, uncovered. Serves 4.

EDINBURG MILL RESTAURANT'S
PUMPKIN MUFFINS

1 teaspoon baking soda
⅓ cup water
1 cup pumpkin, cooked
½ cup oil
2 eggs, beaten
1½ cups sugar

1⅔ cups flour, sifted
½ teaspoon baking powder
¼ teaspoon salt
½ teaspoon cinnamon
½ teaspoon nutmeg

Dissolve baking soda in water. Combine all wet ingredients, mixing thoroughly. Sift all dry ingredients together and combine with wet ingredients, stirring until completely blended. Fill non-stick sprayed muffin tins half full. Bake in 350-degree oven until golden brown, about 30 to 35 minutes. Yields 18 muffins.

EDINBURG MILL RESTAURANT'S BAKED CARROTS

2½ cups carrots, chopped
2 tablespoons onion,
    chopped
2 tablespoons butter
2 eggs, beaten

1 tablespoon flour
1 cup evaporated milk
dash of salt and pepper
¼ teaspoon nutmeg
paprika

Boil carrots until medium tender; drain and mash slightly, leaving carrots lumpy. Combine all ingredients together except paprika. Place in greased casserole dish, sprinkle with paprika and bake in 350-degree oven for 25 to 30 minutes. Serves 4.

WAYSIDE INN
Middletown

WAYSIDE INN

If George Washington didn't sleep here, he should have. A majority of the inn's dining rooms honor our first president. Yes, portraits and prints are the expected homages, but displaying the very stump from the cherry tree that little George chopped does lend an unexpected note of whimsey.

In 1797 the inn was opened for bed and board to travelers of the Black Bear Trail. Some twenty years later, the tavern became a stagecoach stop and relay station. Since schedules fluctuated, the tavern keeper sent a young boy to scan the horizon for approaching stagecoaches. As soon as one was spotted, the boy alerted the cook to rekindle the fire so hungry passengers wouldn't have to wait for refreshment.

Somebody must have been on the alert the day I arrived, as I was no sooner seated in the Portrait Room when a steaming bowl of Peanut Soup was set before me. I enjoyed a lot of good peanut soups in my Virginia travels, but noticed that this savory serving leaned more toward a fresh peanut taste than did the others. A crisp green salad accompanied my Chicken Pot Pie. Huge chunks of chicken are enhanced with herbs grown in their garden at the back of the inn. I also found that a splash of a Virginia rosé bestowed a light yet influential touch to my meal.

For dessert I ordered their famous Carrot Cake, and I must say that it lived up to its delectable reputation. Had I really felt the need to put the brakes on those calories, I could have ordered chilled fresh fruit or Prime Rib sans potatoes.

When I return to the Wayside, I'll opt for dining in the Old Slave Kitchen that was discovered, quite by accident, behind a wall only a few years ago. I want to retreat a century or two sitting by that roaring fireplace as I listen to eighteenth-century music played by strolling balladeers.

The more I think about it, George Washington must have dined here. After all, he is credited with being "first in war, first in peace, and first in the hearts of his countrymen." It only makes sense that fine food was another first in his priorities, and this remarkable old inn has always been known for its fine cuisine and hospitality.

The Wayside Inn is located at 7783 Main Street in Middletown. Meals are served daily. Breakfast is served daily from 7:00 a.m. until 11:30 a.m. Lunch is served from 11:30 a.m. until 3:00 p.m., Monday through Saturday. Dinner is served from 5:00 p.m. until 9:00 p.m., Monday through Thursday, and from 5:00 p.m. until 9:30 p.m. on Friday and Saturday. On Sunday, meals are served from noon until 8:30 p.m. For reservations (recommended) call (703) 869-1797.

WAYSIDE INN'S CARROT CAKE

2 cups sugar
4 eggs
1½ cups oil
2 cups self-rising flour
1½ teaspoons baking soda
2 teaspoons cinnamon

2 junior baby food jars of carrots or 2 cups grated carrots
½ cup black walnuts (optional)

Beat sugar, eggs and oil thoroughly and slowly. Add flour, baking soda and cinnamon to first three ingredients, mixing well. Fold in carrots; add nuts (if desired) and mix until well blended. Bake in sheet cake pan at 350 degrees for 40 minutes. Cool. (Can be cooked in angel food cake pan, baking 10 to 15 minutes longer.) Yields 1 cake.

Carrot Cake Icing:
1 stick margarine or butter
8 ounces cream cheese
1 box confectioners' sugar
1 teaspoon vanilla

¼ to ½ cup of coconut (on top)
sprinkle of black walnuts (on top)

Cream margarine and cream cheese together. Add vanilla. Mix in sugar until mixture is smooth. Spread on cake. Add toppings. Garnish with mint leaves and grated carrots to form flower, if desired. Yields 1 cake.

WAYSIDE INN'S ROAST TURKEY
WITH PEANUT DRESSING

1½ cups finely chopped
  celery
¾ cups finely chopped
  onion
½ cup fresh snipped
  parsley
1 cup butter or margarine
2 cups salted peanuts,
  chopped

1 tablespoon ground sage
1 teaspoon pepper
½ teaspoon salt
12 cups soft bread crumbs
½ cup chicken broth or
  stock
1 12- to 14-pound turkey
cooking oil

In saucepan, sauté celery, onion and parsley in butter or margarine until tender. Stir in peanuts, sage, pepper and salt. Place bread in large mixing bowl and add peanut mixture and chicken broth, mixing well. Rinse turkey; pat dry. Spoon some of the dressing into neck cavity and secure with skewer. Spoon remaining dressing into other cavity; secure and brush turkey breast with cooking oil. Roast (uncovered) in 325-degree oven until meat thermometer registers 185 degrees and drumsticks move easily (about 4½ to 5 hours). Remove and let stand 15 minutes. Serves 24.

WAYSIDE INN'S PRIME RIB

5-pound prime rib
water to cover
2 teaspoons salt
1½ teaspoons pepper
1 teaspoon rosemary

1½ teaspoons sage
1 garlic clove, chopped
1 onion, quartered
1 celery stalk, sliced
1 carrot stick, sliced

Cover prime rib with water. Add vegetables and seasonings and bake in a 350-degree oven for 20 minutes per pound of rib; if a well-done rib is desired, cook longer. Serves 6.

THE INN AT LITTLE WASHINGTON
Washington

THE INN AT LITTLE WASHINGTON

For me, experiencing The Inn at Little Washington is akin to looking through a glass prism, watching patterns of light refract to give each ray its own unique splendor.

The exterior, originally a garage in the early 1900s, does not even hint of the interior's elegance.

Once inside, however, the vaulted ceiling designed in a fresco collage reminded me of a Byzantine museum transformed into an exquisite French restaurant. In the main dining room huge, ruffled, peach taffeta lamp shades hang from the ceiling to accent each table set with unusual fresh flowers.

While absorbing the ambiance, my appetizer of Crab and Spinach Timbale was presented under a bell-shaped glass. This delicacy exceeded the expectations my dinner companions, John and Julia Bize, had engendered. Before the entrées, our palettes were exotically cleansed with Fresh Fruit Sorbets.

My entrée of Sweetbreads, sautéed with three mustards and alternating layers of snow peas, was artistically designed to appear as a kaleidoscope. The taste was as fulfilling as its visual appeal. Julia let me sample her Duckling with Shenandoah Apples, an entrée which places duck in an entirely new category. I also snitched a bite of John's succulent Veal Chausseur.

Desserts offered even further visual wonders. I mean, have you ever seen chocolate made to stand up in the shape of a lace fan? Even the Coeur à la Crème was presented in a heart shape and served with a scrumptious Raspberry Sauce.

Manager Reinhardt Lynch and Chef Patrick O'Connell behave as if it were effortless. "It's important to appear effortless," said O'Connell. "For instance, one day I was working outside over a brazier when a twister swept the brazier into the sky and scattered chicken over the entire area. Then rain poured, causing a power failure, and dinner had to be cooked by flashlight! We simply added more candles, and the guests never realized our catastrophes."

Compromise simply is not a word in their vocabulary; excellence is, which makes this extraordinary French restaurant a connoisseur's euphoria.

The Inn at Little Washington is located on the corner of Middle and Main Streets in Washington. Dinner is served from 6:00 p.m. until 9:30 p.m., Wednesday through Friday, 5:30 p.m. until 10:30 p.m. on Saturday, and 4:00 p.m. until 9:30 p.m. on Sunday. The restaurant is closed in January. For reservations (required) call (703) 675-3800.

THE INN AT LITTLE WASHINGTON'S CRAB AND SPINACH TIMBALE

Crab Mousse:

½ pound backfin crabmeat
¼ cup heavy cream
1 teaspoon lemon juice
½ teaspoon mustard
½ teaspoon celery salt

dash of cayenne
½ teaspoon salt
½ teaspoon pepper
2 eggs

In a bowl, combine crabmeat, cream, lemon juice, mustard, celery salt, cayenne, salt and pepper. Beat eggs. Blend beaten eggs into crabmeat mixture and refrigerate.

Spinach Timbale:

1 pound fresh spinach
3 tablespoons unsalted
   butter
2 tablespoons flour
¾ cup milk
½ cup heavy cream

1 teaspoon salt
freshly ground pepper to
   taste
⅛ teaspoon grated nutmeg
3 large eggs
pimientos cut into stars

Boil spinach in salted water. Drain, then cool in cold water. Drain and chop finely. Make a roux with butter and flour. Add milk, cream, salt, pepper and nutmeg. Bring mixture to boil. Remove from heat. Stir in spinach. Allow mixture to cool slightly and beat in eggs. Half fill eight buttered molds or muffin tins and place tins in shallow pan of cold water. Bake in 375-degree oven 25 to 30 minutes or until set. Cool.

Run a knife around edge to unmold. Place on serving plates. Spoon mousse on top and garnish with star-shaped pimiento. Serves 8.

THE INN AT LITTLE WASHINGTON'S
COEUR À LA CRÈME WITH RASPBERRY SAUCE

Filling:

8 ounces cream cheese, softened	**1 teaspoon vanilla**
	1 teaspoon lemon juice
⅔ cup sifted confectioners' sugar	**1 teaspoon framboise or kirsch**
1¼ cups heavy cream	

Using an electric mixer, beat cream cheese until smooth; blend in sugar, a few tablespoons at a time, scraping down sides of bowl. In a chilled bowl, whip cream until stiff. Gently fold half of whipped cream into cream cheese mixture. Add vanilla, lemon juice and framboise, and gently fold in remaining whipped cream. Line either six ½-cup *coeur à la crème* molds, a 3-cup mold with holes or a closely woven basket with a double thickness of dampened cotton cheesecloth. Fill with mixture and cover with cheesecloth and refrigerate overnight. Remove cheesecloth and unmold by inverting onto serving plates. Spoon Raspberry Sauce (recipe below) over each dessert. Garnish with whole berries. Serves 6.

Note: *Coeur à la Crème* molds have tiny holes in the bottom to allow liquids to drain from the cheese.

Raspberry Sauce:

2 pints raspberries (or strawberries), hulled and washed	**1 tablespoon framboise (raspberry brandy) or kirsch**
½ cup sugar	**1 teaspoon lemon juice**

Reserve ¼ cup berries for garnish. In blender, purée the remaining berries, sugar, framboise and lemon juice. Strain through a fine sieve.

SIXTY-SEVEN WATERLOO
Warrenton

SIXTY-SEVEN WATERLOO

Can you imagine spending eighty hours refinishing an 1838 spindle-style mantel? That was just one of the projects undertaken by Philip and Alison Harway when they purchased the antebellum mansion built by General Eppa Hunton at number Sixty-Seven Waterloo. Today a portrait of the general, acclaimed at Gettysburg and elected to Congress in 1873, hangs above this mantel.

In 1908, the home became the residence of artist Richard Brooke, who was appointed vice-principal of the School of Art at the Corcoran in Washington. Miraculously, the home escaped the Great Fire of 1909 that destroyed not only Brooke's studio and valuable art collection but the entire western part of Warrenton.

After many months of renovating the original wood floors and walls and tracing down the family portraits that now hang in the upstairs sitting room and stairway, the Harways opened a restaurant serving traditional French cuisine. This success led them to transform the original slave quarters at the back of the home into a rustic wood tavern, whimsically named Napoleon's.

It was one of those heaven-sent, clear spring days when I dined on their outdoor patio above Napoleon's. That meal was my special event of the day, as Chef Robert Chiovoloni joins the Harways and me in the philosophy that eating must be more than a habit to satisfy basic needs. True exponents of culinary art were placed before me.

The spectacle began with a subtle, creamy Mousse de Foie (goose liver) and a spicy Green Peppercorn Pâté served on their homebaked Honey Whole Wheat Bread and crackers. I selected an unpretentious white chardonnay from one of their bimonthly wine tastings, which proved the right choice for my own taste-testing of their saucy Crabmeat with Hazelnuts, a homemade Pasta stuffed with herbs and cheeses and the best Asparagus on Puff Pastry that I've tasted.

Then came the dessert masterpieces. The Chocolate Amaretto Mousse fashioned into tiers of ruffled chocolate lace looked as if it should have been framed rather than devoured. This sinfully succulent creation competed with a Strawberry Charlotte that artistically tucked a mousse into its center.

This restaurant takes such pleasure in presentation that they welcome the challenge (when notified in advance) to prepare diet menus that deliver the same appeal as their more affluent dishes.

Sixty-Seven Waterloo is located in Warrenton at Sixty-Seven Waterloo. Dinner is served Tuesday through Saturday from 5:30 p.m. until 9:30 p.m., and on Sunday from 3:00 p.m. until 9:30 p.m. For reservations (recommended) call (703) 347-1200.

SIXTY-SEVEN WATERLOO'S CRABMEAT WITH HAZELNUTS

4 ounces hazelnuts
1 pound backfin crabmeat
2 tablespoons hazelnut oil
1½ teaspoons sherry
  vinegar

1 teaspoon fresh coriander
salt and pepper to taste
lettuce leaves

Chop the hazelnuts coarsely, removing the skins, and roast until brown. Mix hazelnuts with carefully cleaned crabmeat. Dress mixture with hazelnut oil, sherry vinegar and coriander, and salt and pepper to taste. Toss together very gently in order not to break up the lumps of crabmeat. (If unable to find sherry vinegar, mix equal portions of sherry and wine vinegar.) Serve on bed of lettuce. Serves 8 to 10.

SIXTY-SEVEN WATERLOO'S ASPARAGUS ON PUFF PASTRY

4 sheets puff pastry
(Pepperidge Farm)
1 egg white

1 pound fresh asparagus
Beurre Blanc (recipe
follows)

Early in the day, roll out puff pastry sheets into 4-inch by 1½-inch squares. Brush 4 squares with egg white and score. Spray baking sheet with non-stick spray and bake according to package directions. Remove from oven, split and return to 200-degree oven for an hour until squares are dried out. Reserve. Steam asparagus and place on puff pastry squares; drizzle with Beurre Blanc. Serves 4.

SIXTY-SEVEN WATERLOO'S BEURRE BLANC

1 shallot, minced
1 pound softened butter
¼ cup white wine
1 tablespoon wine vinegar

½ lemon, juice only
¼ cup heavy cream
salt and pepper to taste

In skillet over medium heat, soften shallot in 2 tablespoons of the butter, but do not brown. Add wine, vinegar and lemon juice and reduce liquid by 75 percent; add cream and reduce until "fish eyes" appear, indicating that cream is sufficiently concentrated. Slowly whisk in softened butter over gentle heat, not boiling. Season with salt and pepper. Can be used with other vegetables and meats. Store in refrigerator for other uses. Yields approximately 2 cups.

THE RED FOX TAVERN
Middleburg

THE RED FOX TAVERN

George Washington, General Jeb Stuart, Colonel John Mosby, President John F. Kennedy and John Adair have all dined at The Red Fox Tavern. Not familiar with John Adair? Perhaps you've mistakenly heard of him as "Monty," the Confederate Civil War ghost. Recently, Monty made himself so visible to an attractive, mature lady overnighting at the tavern that she snapped his picture. When developed, a parapsychologist and photographer examined the photos and concluded that an entity was indeed captured on film.

Weeks later the lady destroyed the film in an effort to free herself of Monty's presence. Finally, a medium was called who made contact with Monty. The piqued spirit announced that he was John Adair, not Monty, and explained that he had fallen in love with the beautiful woman. The Confederate soldier had traveled home with the lady because, in his time period, it was not safe for a lady to travel alone. The spirit reluctantly agreed to leave when told that the lady was married. So, if staying at the Red Fox, remember their ghost has a penchant for older, attractive women.

Unfortunately, I missed meeting John Adair. Nonetheless, lunching in Joseph Chinn's 1728 ordinary was more than ample compensation. I sat across from the bar allegedly used as an operating table when the tavern functioned as a hospital during the Civil War. Here my taste buds experienced Chef Michael Gagne's heavenly Brie in Filo with Pistachio Nut Butter, accompanied by a vibrant Folonara rosé that was perfect with Gagne's hearty Red Fox Country Soup. Many of these two-hundred-year-old recipes found their origin here in the nation's foremost area for fox hunting and thoroughbred horse racing. Others, such as the divine Duckling Somerset, are recent adaptations. My meal was concluded with a light, yet tart, Raspberry Champagne Sorbet and a taste of their fantastic homemade Apple Butter Ice Cream.

If you don't intend to burn your calories riding to the hounds, you might choose to lunch on their Watercress and

Endive Salad or a Vegetable Platter. At dinner, the Entrecote (fish broiled in wine) should keep you fit and scrumptiously satisfied.

On my next trip I hope to stay at the Red Fox, sample their Pecan Waffle for breakfast and, who knows, maybe engage John Adair in a friendly tête à tête.

The Red Fox Tavern is located at 2 East Washington Street in Middleburg. Meals are served daily. Breakfast is from 8:00 a.m. until 10:30 a.m.; lunch is from 11:30 a.m. until 2:30 p.m. (except Sunday). Dinner is from 6:00 p.m. until 9:00 p.m., Monday through Friday, from 5:00 p.m. until 9:30 p.m. on Saturday and noon until 8:00 p.m. on Sunday. For reservations (recommended) call (703) 687-6301.

THE RED FOX TAVERN'S BRIE IN FILO WITH PISTACHIO NUT BUTTER

filo pastry, 2 leaves
¼ stick clarified butter
Brie, 1 tin

Pistachio Nut Butter (recipe follows)

Lay out filo dough and brush with clarified butter. Place 2 ounces Brie on each filo leaf and add Pistachio Nut Butter over Brie. Fold filo into thirds and seal with clarified butter. Place on greased cookie sheet and put in 450-degree oven until golden brown (a few minutes). Don't overcook. Slice while hot. Serves 3 to 4.

Pistachio Nut Butter:
2 ounces raw pistachios, shelled and peeled
1 stick unsalted butter

salt and white pepper to taste

On cookie sheet, roast pistachios at 275 degrees until golden brown. Process in food processor or blender with steel blade until fine. Blend with softened butter. Salt and pepper (white) to taste.

THE RED FOX TAVERN'S RASPBERRY
CHAMPAGNE SORBET

4 pints fresh raspberries or
   5 10-ounce packages of
   frozen
2 cups extra fine sugar,
   divided

1 bottle of champagne
1 whole egg, unshelled, for
   testing
juice of 1 lemon
mint for garnish

If using fresh berries, crush slightly and sprinkle with one cup of sugar and let sit overnight in refrigerator. (Omit marinating overnight if using frozen berries.) The next day drain the juice and discard the pulp. Add the champagne to the raspberry juice and test for sugar density by floating an unshelled egg in the liquid. Continue to add sugar until egg surfaces—at least a half-inch in diameter of the egg should be showing. (When this occurs there is enough sugar.) Remove egg. Add lemon juice and pour mixture into a stainless steel bowl and place in freezer. Stir about once every hour until frozen, or process mixture in ice cream freezer according to machine's directions. Serve garnished with mint. Yields 3 quarts.

KING'S COURT TAVERN
Leesburg

KING'S COURT
TAVERN

When you hear the bell ring at King's Court, it is signaling the opening or closing of the restaurant. A hundred and fifty years ago, when the first proprietor, Mr. Philmore, operated the building as The Country Store, the same bell was used to inform the towns-people of the store's opening and closing. Back in those days much of the store's business was done through bartering; so today, when possible, services are bartered for food and refreshment.

I find that a very appealing way to do business, and in most instances, it's a lot more fun than the monetary transactions most of us are saddled with using.

Arriving at King's Court for a late lunch, I sat at an old wooden table across from a full-service bar. The bar is separated from the dining area, and retains the store's original red oak gingerbread ceiling border. The room is reminiscent of a colonial tavern with the Williamsburg-gray wainscotting that panels the walls. The upper half of the walls are dotted with antique prints, many of which were purchased from Arthur Godfrey's farm. The original, wide windowpanes admit just the right amount of light.

Whenever possible, I prefer to sample a number of items on a restaurant's menu. That way, I can supply more informed suggestions and know which recipes to request. I began with the Potato Soup, made fresh each day, and knew instantly that I wanted to include that recipe for home use. Then I taste-tested their Reuben and Monte Cristo sandwiches, but wound up asking for their London Broil. My recommendation for dessert would have to be the Cheesecake.

The bar offers a large variety of cocktails or a nice selection of wines and beers.

In the evening you can enjoy live entertainment, usually folk singers and musicians from many different countries.

It would be a real treat to return to Leesburg in mid-August when the main streets are blocked off for two days for a colonial celebration. Merrymaking includes clogging, old time music and the display of a variety of colonial crafts.

As a matter of fact, the tin wall sconces at King's Court were fashioned at one of the past summer events. So, mid-August in Leesburg is a good date to put on your calendar when planning a trip through this beautiful countryside.

King's Court is located at 2 C West Loudoun Street in Leesburg. Lunch is served Monday through Saturday from 11:30 a.m. until 2:00 p.m. Dinner is served from 2:00 p.m. until 10:00 p.m., Monday through Saturday, and 11:30 a.m. until 10:00 p.m. on Sunday. The bar is open until 1:00 a.m. on Friday and Saturday. Reservations are not accepted, but if you need to call, the phone number is (703) 777-7747.

KING'S COURT TAVERN'S POTATO SOUP

2 tablespoons margarine
2 cups potatoes, peeled and
   chopped
¼ cup fresh parsley,
   chopped
½ cup onion, chopped
1 bay leaf
1 teaspoon salt
1 teaspoon pepper

2½ cups chicken stock or
   broth
2 to 3 cups water
1 cup half and half
3 tablespoons flour
½ cup sour cream
3 to 4 teaspoons chives,
   chopped

Melt margarine in a large pot and sauté potatoes, chopped into cubes, with parsley, onion, bay leaf, salt and pepper. Add chicken stock (or broth) and water, reduce heat to medium and cook for 10 to 12 minutes. Cover and reduce heat to low and cook for 18 to 20 minutes. In a small bowl mix half and half with flour until lumps disappear. Pour into soup, stirring to prevent lumps from forming, and simmer for 30 minutes. Before serving, stir in sour cream and heat through. Sprinkle with chives. Serves 8 to 10.

KING'S COURT TAVERN'S LONDON BROIL

1 1½- to 2-pound flank
  steak
1 cup salad oil
4 tablespoons wine vinegar
¾ teaspoon oregano

¼ teaspoon salt
¼ teaspoon pepper
1 onion, diced
½ pound large mushroom
  caps

Trim flank steak very close, removing all skin, membrane and fat, and place in a large square or rectangular glass dish. Combine salad oil, vinegar, oregano, salt, pepper, onion and mushroom caps and pour over steak. Marinate in refrigerator at least 2 hours or longer. Remove steak from marinade and place on broiler pan. Use pre-heated broiler rack closest to heating unit. Broil for 4 to 5 minutes on each side until meat reaches rare to medium stage. Do not overcook. Remove and slice steak in very thin diagonal slices about ¼-inch thick and serve with Bordelaise Sauce (recipe below). Serves 4.

Bordelaise Sauce:

2 tablespoons butter
1 small onion, chopped
2 shallots
1 cup red wine

1 clove garlic, minced
¼ cup wine vinegar
1 cup brown sauce
chopped parsley

Melt butter in skillet, and sauté onions and shallots until transparent. Combine garlic and vinegar. Add wine and garlic/vinegar mixture. Reduce liquid to half by boiling, and add brown sauce. Serve over meat and garnish with chopped parsley. Yields 1½ cups.

LAUREL BRIGADE INN
Leesburg

LAUREL BRIGADE INN

It is a little-known fact that the Confederate Laurel Brigade, led by Colonel Elijah V. White, never surrendered. When White saw the happenings at Appomattox, he led his troops off to Lynchburg, refusing to take any part of defeat. Prior to Appomattox, the brigade was recognized for gallant conduct, and they signified this distinction with a sprig of laurel in their hatbands. The new name selected for this converted 1766 ordinary is in honor of the brave brigade.

Ellen Flippo Wall told me her father purchased the inn in 1945 because it would have been demolished to make way for a discount store. That was years before preserving the past was championed as an admired undertaking.

Roy Flippo worked to preserve the structure's architectural integrity by repairing the combination stone and brick wall that divides the kitchen from the main dining room. The wall was hastily built in 1825 in a special celebration held here for Lafayette, who was visiting President Monroe in nearby Washington.

It was, by all reports, a very festive day. One of the guests became tipsy and disappeared. In the excitement over his absence, the partygoers mistook the mewing of a cat who had fallen into the well for the cries of the missing, tipsy guest. Ah yes, those were spirited times.

The well is still in the inn's beautiful garden, which is governed by a massive osage orange tree. Flowers abound here, including a host of peonies that were planted around 1854. This soothing view made me insist on a table overlooking the garden.

Lunching at Laurel Brigade was like visiting my grandmother. She used to put all the foods cooked during the week on the table at every meal. The food kept reappearing until it was eaten because everyone knows, "It's a sin to waste."

No, they don't serve leftovers. Nevertheless, I wasted not one single bite, remembering how similar their homemade Curried Chicken was to my grandmother's. Their Beef Stew was another good and hearty dish, and the Avocado Mousse made an unusual salad offering. However, I was partial to their Chicken Pot Pie, bountifully laced with hefty chicken chunks.

Apple Brown Betty with Hard Sauce is their dessert specialty, and I was tickled to get that recipe.

Although iced tea suited my mood that day, they do offer a modest selection of wine and alcoholic beverages.

As I was leaving, Mrs. Wall pointed out that the hardware on the front door was installed upside down. So, for the past two hundred and seventeen years it's been necessary to insert the door key in reverse. Just another amusing architectural eccentricity she wouldn't dream of altering.

The Laurel Brigade is located at 20 West Market Street in Leesburg. Lunch is served Tuesday through Saturday from noon until 2:00 p.m., and dinner is from 5:00 p.m. until 8:00 p.m. Sunday dinner is served from noon until 7:00 p.m. For reservations (recommended) call (703) 777-1010.

LAUREL BRIGADE INN'S CURRIED CHICKEN

1 3- to 4-pound stewing
  chicken
1 gallon water
6 tablespoons butter
1 cup onion, finely chopped
1 cup celery, finely chopped
1 cup apple, finely chopped
3 tablespoons flour

1 tablespoon curry powder
2 teaspoons turmeric
2 teaspoons marjoram
salt and pepper to taste
rice (follow package
  directions)
parsley for garnish

Cook the chicken in boiling water until meat separates easily from the bone. Remove the chicken and let liquid reduce. Cube chicken and set aside. In a skillet, melt 3 tablespoons of butter and sauté onions, celery and apple for 7 to 10 minutes. In a saucepan, form a roux with remaining butter and flour. Slowly add about a cup of the reduced chicken liquid to the roux, and stir to combine. Add sautéed vegetables and apples, and season with curry powder, turmeric and marjoram. Salt and pepper to taste. Simmer for 10 minutes. Add the cubed chicken and simmer another 5 minutes. Serve over a bed of parsley-garnished rice. Serves 8.

LAUREL BRIGADE INN'S AVOCADO MOUSSE

1 tablespoon unflavored
  gelatin
2 tablespoons cold water
1 3-ounce package lime
  gelatin

2 cups hot water
1 cup mashed avocado
½ cup mayonnaise
½ cup whipping cream,
  whipped

Dissolve unflavored gelatin in cold water. Dissolve lime gelatin in hot water. Mix gelatins together and chill until slightly thickened. Fold in avocado, mayonnaise and whipped cream. Spoon into 4-cup mold and chill. Serves 6 to 8.

LAUREL BRIGADE INN'S APPLE BROWN BETTY

¼ cup butter
2 cups bread crumbs,
  toasted
4 cups apples, peeled and
  sliced
¼ cup raisins
¼ cup brown sugar

⅛ teaspoon salt
¼ teaspoon nutmeg
1 teaspoon cinnamon
1 tablespoon lemon juice
1 teaspoon vanilla
½ cup apple juice

Melt butter and place in a casserole dish. Add alternate layers of bread crumbs, apples, raisins and brown sugar. Sprinkle with salt, nutmeg and cinnamon. Combine lemon juice, vanilla and apple juice and pour over top. End with a layer of bread crumbs. Bake in a 350-degree oven for 40 minutes. Serve with Hard Sauce (recipe below). Serves 6 to 8.

Hard Sauce:

½ stick margarine
1½ cups confectioners'
  sugar

½ cup apple jack brandy

Place softened margarine, sugar and brandy in blender and blend until smooth. Serve small amount over Apple Brown Betty.

EVANS FARM INN
McLean

EVANS FARM INN

Dreamily sequestered on forty acres of rolling green countryside sits Evans Farm Inn. I first saw this eighteenth-century farm on a day in early spring when my eyes were met with an artist's palette of azaleas and blossoming fruit trees.

True to its farm claim, rows of vegetables and herbs were in their sprouting stages. Seeing a restaurant's growing vegetable garden gives you an idea of what to expect from their food.

As I continued to tour the grounds, I found an old, log smokehouse, a stable turned gift shop and a number of animals for small children to pet, including a llama.

I then came upon the traditional, old cookhouse where a rather romantic celebration occurred recently. A husband surprised his wife on their eighteenth wedding anniversary by booking a candlelight dinner for the two of them in this quaint old building where their wedding reception had been held.

My tour concluded at the main restaurant, constructed from century-old materials salvaged from churches, mansions and barns. These authentic "oddments," as they are called, lend colonial authenticity to the rooms.

The ingenuity of colonial design is represented in the tremendous antique fireplace, still hung with heavy chains of varying lengths that were used to cook a number of dishes simultaneously.

I sipped a good, old-fashioned Mint Julep in this large, homey main dining room before moving downstairs to have dinner in The Sitting Duck, a casual English pub-styled dining room. The moment I walked through the door, I heard a group crowded around the piano singing *Balling the Jack*.

Luckily, I was able to sample many of the foods that have made Evans Farm Inn famous. Served by period-costumed waitresses, my meal began with a unique Onion Soup cooked with paprika-seasoned flour and Provolone cheese. This luscious appetizer was followed by Danish-imported Baby

Spareribs, said to be the favorite of Washington Redskins player, Dave Butz. Another inspired sampling is their Seafood Newberg. This dish is usually their buffet staple, owing to its popularity, along with an exceptional Asparagus and Pea Casserole.

For dessert I sampled the super rich Chocolate Cheesecake, the yummy Apple Walnut Cake, made without preservatives, and their esteemed, old Virginia recipe—Apple Crisp.

To enrich my meal, I enjoyed a subtle Riesling while reading a wine list that quotes Plato: "When a man drinks wine at dinner, he begins to feel better pleased with himself." I've noticed that women realize a similar experience; but, in my opinion, a visit to this revitalizing inn is sufficient tonic to put anyone in a better mood.

Evans Farm Inn is located at 1696 Chain Bridge Road in McLean. Lunch is served from 11:30 a.m. until 2:30 p.m., Monday through Saturday; dinner is served from 5:00 p.m. until 9:00 p.m., Monday through Thursday, and 5:00 p.m. until 10:00 p.m. on Friday and Saturday. Sunday dinner is served from noon until 9:00 p.m. For reservations (recommended), call (703) 356-8000.

EVANS FARM INN'S CHICKEN BARBARA

3 double chicken breasts	1 large onion, sliced
2 cloves garlic	salt and pepper to taste
6 celery stalks, with leaves	dash of rosemary

Place chicken breasts in steamer and add 1 minced garlic clove, 4-inch celery pieces with leaves and onion; steam. When half steamed, season with salt, pepper and rosemary. Steam until cooked, and cool. Remove skin from chicken breasts and cut each chicken breast in half (six pieces in all). Rub each chicken portion with the other cut clove of garlic. Dip chicken in Waffle Batter (recipe below) and fry in deep fat at 375 degrees until golden brown. Serve by placing each chicken portion on top of ¼ cup of Lemon Cream Sauce (recipe below). Garnish with watercress. Serves 6.

Waffle Batter:

1¾ cups sifted flour	½ teaspoon baking soda
1¼ teaspoons baking powder	2 small eggs, separated
	1¼ cups buttermilk

Sift dry ingredients and set aside. Beat egg yolks until frothy. Add buttermilk and beat again. Whip egg whites until stiff. Add flour mixture to buttermilk mixture and beat to a smooth consistency. Fold in egg whites carefully.

Lemon Cream Sauce:

1 tablespoon butter	1 cup light cream or milk
1 tablespoon flour	1 tablespoon lemon juice

In skillet melt butter and add flour, making a roux. Add cream slowly, stirring to incorporate. Add lemon juice and blend until smooth.

EVANS FARM INN'S ASPARAGUS AND PEA CASSEROLE

10½-ounce can of asparagus	½ cup sharp Cheddar cheese, grated
8½-ounce can tiny peas	
8-ounce can water chestnuts	2 tablespoons butter
10¾-ounce can mushroom soup	½ cup bread crumbs, fine

Drain vegetables thoroughly. Slice chestnuts very thin. Grease a casserole dish and place a layer of asparagus, a layer of peas, a layer of water chestnuts, a layer of mushroom soup and a layer of cheese. Repeat layers, ending with cheese on top. Bake in a 325-degree oven 25 to 30 minutes. Melt butter and combine with bread crumbs and spread mixture over top of casserole. Return to oven for 8 to 10 minutes until brown on top. Serves 4.

GADSBY'S TAVERN
Alexandria

GADSBY'S TAVERN

As I stood on the front door-step of Gadsby's Tavern, I tried to picture how it must have looked to General George Washington, standing there for the last time, reviewing his troops. Even though Alexandria is quaint, you can't deny the intrusion of the twentieth century.

Inside is another story, and if you visit in the evening, it may not be clear which century you've entered. Playing the lute guitar, John Douglas Hall is apt to be singing a Scot song of the eighteenth century, or perhaps interpreting the daily news of the Revolution for the folks who have come to Gadsby's to take their repast.

Built in 1792 by Charles and Ann Mason, Gadsby's four stories were constructed as the City Hotel. In those days, this excellent example of Georgian architecture was considered a veritable skyscraper. The interior was done in such refined taste that no less than six United States presidents have used it for receptions and grand balls. The Blue Ballroom, now used for dining, seemed quite small to me, especially when you think that such political notables as George Washington, Marquis de Lafayette, John Paul Jones, John Adams, Thomas Jefferson and James Madison were either doing the minuet or a little "do-si-doing" around this floor during one administration or another.

It is, however, ideal for dining, and patrons today can enjoy many of the same fine foods that our nation's most prominent people loved.

Gadsby's makes their own Sangria and offers other unique alcoholic beverages, including Madeira, a liquid George Washington used for soaking his dentures. I found that a glass of their homebrew is a pleasant way to begin your meal. I ordered the Turkey Devonshire, a rich and creamy open-faced sandwich, and a delicious Clam Chowder for lunch. They also serve their famed Sally Lunn Bread. This is a recipe that was later tested by my mother, who wrote, "I never should have tried this—your father insists that I bake it as a standard food item!"

For a lighter dish, and a good choice in this seaport community, try their Shrimp and Scallops sautéed in a little lemon butter and white wine.

Desserts at Gadsby's are in tune with eighteenth century ingredients, and I chose Washington's favorite, the Buttermilk Pie. It has a satiny-smooth texture and slips down like silk, which makes it difficult to stop at one piece.

Gadsby's is located on 138 North Royal Street in Alexandria. Meals are served daily. Lunch is from 11:30 a.m. until 3:30 p.m., and dinner is from 5:30 p.m., with no one seated after 9:00 p.m., Monday through Friday. On Sunday, brunch is served from 11:00 a.m., with the last seating at 3:00 p.m., and dinner is from 5:30 p.m. until 9:00 p.m. For reservations (required) call (703) 548-1288.

GADSBY'S TAVERN'S SALLY LUNN BREAD

1 cup milk	**⅓ cup sugar**
½ cup shortening	**½ teaspoon salt**
¼ cup water	**2 packages active dry yeast**
4 cups flour, sifted	**3 eggs**

Grease two loaf pans. Heat milk, shortening and water to 115 degrees (water should be warm but not hot; shortening need not melt). Blend 1⅓ cups flour, sugar, salt and dry yeast in mixing bowl. Blend warm liquids into flour mix. Beat at medium speed for 2 minutes, scraping sides of bowl. Gradually add ⅔ cup of the remaining flour and the eggs. Beat at high speed for 2 minutes. Add remaining 2 cups of flour and mix (may have to be mixed by hand). Cover, let rise in warm, draft-free place until double in bulk, about 1 hour and 15 minutes. Beat dough down with spatula or at lowest speed with an electric mixer and turn into greased pans. Cover and let rise about 30 minutes in a warm, draft-free place until increased in bulk by one-third to one-half. Bake for 40 to 50 minutes. Yields 2 loaves.

GADSBY'S TAVERN'S BUTTERMILK PIE

2 eggs
2 cups buttermilk
2 cups sugar

8 teaspoons flour
¾ teaspoon lemon extract
1 9-inch deep dish pie crust

In mixing bowl, combine eggs and buttermilk and beat until well mixed. Add sugar and flour gradually, beating until thoroughly incorporated. Add lemon extract and mix only to blend through. Pour into pie crust and bake in 350-degree oven for 30 to 40 minutes. Cool. Yields 1 pie.

GADSBY'S TAVERN'S TURKEY DEVONSHIRE

¾-pound cooked turkey
6 slices bacon
2 tablespoons butter
3 tablespoons flour
1 cup milk

¾ cup Swiss cheese, grated
¼ cup white wine
salt and pepper to taste
4 slices bread, toasted
4 slices tomato

Slice turkey and set aside. In skillet, fry bacon and set aside. In separate skillet, melt butter over medium heat and stir in flour, making a roux. Stir until all lumps are blended into smooth consistency. Add milk and cheese; raise heat and bring to a boil and cook until sauce reaches thick consistency. Remove from heat and stir in wine, salt and pepper. Return to heat and stir until evenly blended. On a baking sheet, place toast and cover evenly with turkey; pour cheese sauce over top. Place a tomato slice and 1½ slices of crumbled bacon over each. Broil for approximately 1 to 2 minutes. Serves 4.

Note: Excellent for leftover turkey.

KINGS LANDING
Alexandria

KINGS LANDING I magine not being able to dine in a restaurant that has not first been checked by the secret service for security. Security checks are routine at Kings Landing, as this restaurant is on the preferred list of many Washington dignitaries.

Not long ago, after thoroughly sizing up all of the restaurant's five dining rooms, navy intelligence officers informed the management that there was only one position, at one table, in one specific dining room, that was safely out of the line of fire.

Oh well, I suppose dignitaries get used to it, but I would hate not having the freedom to wander into this old seaport restaurant on my own.

Built before the Civil War, the building served as a warehouse in what was considered, before urban renewal, a rather disreputable section of town.

Although the building goes back over a hundred years, only the exposed Flemish bond brick suggests the building's age. There is an appealing view of the Potomac River from the upstairs main dining area where I lunched beneath a huge skylight. Centering the room's ceiling, the skylight seems to bloom with a veritable forest of green plants hanging over a fountain.

As you might expect with a waterfront view, the cuisine is heavily influenced by fresh seafood. Not forgotten, though, are the tastes familiar to Virginians, so the Landing is equally well-known for such Southern specialties as its subtly satisfying Pumpkin Soup. One sip of this wonderful soup, and it was slated for the recipe section.

This appetizer was followed by a sea lover's favorite called Clams Casino and a taste of their very rich Liver Pâté on a slice of freshly baked bread.

When my entrée of Seafood Newberg arrived, swimming with shrimp, scallops and salmon in a lovely cream sauce, I had to break my taste-testing rule and have more than one bite.

The wine list has a strong French influence, and I especially enjoyed a 1981 Riesling from their wine cellar.

If you are interested in something on the light side, I would suggest their Salmon Frais Grille (skipping the Bearnaise sauce) or a most unusual Yogurt Soup.

If traveling that route you should think of coffee or tea instead of their famous Floating Island dessert, or the Chocolate Mousse or Strawberry Tart. All looked wonderful, but I figured that I'd better take a dessert rain check for a thinner day.

Perhaps that thinner day will be an evening when jazz pianist Tony Satarese is playing. I'll be sure to make a point of having a light dinner so I can appreciate his artistry along with one of their appealing desserts.

Kings Landing is located at 121 South Union Street in (Old Town) Alexandria. Lunch is served from 11:30 a.m. until 2:30 p.m. Monday through Saturday. Dinner is served from 6:30 p.m. until 10:00 p.m. Monday through Saturday. On Sunday, brunch is served from noon until 3:00 p.m., and dinner is served from 6:00 p.m. until 9:00 p.m. For reservations (preferred) call (703) 836-7010.

KINGS LANDING'S SEAFOOD IN CREAM SAUCE

1¼ sticks butter	2 cups fish stock
1 pound fresh mushrooms, quartered	dash of cayenne
	8 tablespoons flour
2 cups white wine	1½ pounds scallops
3 shallots, chopped	½ pound tiny shrimp, cleaned
salt and pepper to taste	
1 gallon mussels in shells	

In a skillet melt ¼ stick of butter over high heat and sauté mushrooms and set aside. To large pot add 1 cup wine, shallots, salt, pepper and mussels. Steam until mussels open—about 5 minutes. Remove mussels from shells, being careful to reserve mussel liquid. Put mussel liquid in saucepan with

1 cup wine, fish stock and cayenne. Boil for 4 minutes. Lower heat and cook until liquid is reduced to half. Meanwhile, melt remaining butter in small saucepan and add flour, stirring to form a paste. Add flour mixture to mussel liquid, and cook for 5 minutes. Add scallops, mussels, mushrooms and shrimp, and cook for additional 5 minutes. Serves 10 to 12.

KINGS LANDING'S PUMPKIN SOUP

1 cup pumpkin, ripe and
  seedless
¼ cup chicken stock or
  broth
½ of large potato, peeled
  and diced
½ medium Spanish onion,
  chopped
3 tablespoons butter

1 to 2 slices bacon,
  uncooked and chopped
salt and pepper to taste
½ cup water (or enough
  water to cover
  ingredients)
dash of nutmeg
1 tablespoon creme sherry
1 cup half and half

In a large pot, combine all ingredients except sherry and half and half. Cook over medium heat for about 5 minutes. Reduce heat to simmer and cook approximately 30 minutes. Remove and place in mixing bowl or blender and mix until consistency is smooth. Return to low heat, add sherry and half and half, and stir until heated through. Serves 4 to 6.

PORTNER'S
Alexandria

PORTNER'S

At Portner's, the wine is kept in the elevator. Since everyone knows that firemen slide down poles, the elevator at this old fire station was installed during the building's renovation. If your relatives happened by Portner's in 1883, when the building was Columbia County Number Four, they may have joined the town council in chasing hogs off the street to make way for the new steam fire engine. Or, they could have had business on the northern end of Asaph Street with the Robert Portner Brewing Company, which, incidentally, is what the restaurant is named after.

Whatever their venture, I'll bet it was not as gastronomically unique and pleasing as mine. I happened by Portner's just before the lunch hour. Their front window displays a hanging Tiffany stained-glass lamp fashioned into a butterfly. The morning sun's penetration diffused a spray of color through the prisms, causing a captivating effect. Later, I learned that this lamp had been made for the Saint Louis World's Fair and was just one of the many rare antiques comprising Portner's fascinating décor.

The restaurant has four floors with four distinctly dissimilar personalities. Hence, you could dine on separate floors four days in a row and never experience the same atmosphere. From the top floor's Wannamaker Room, done in the Gothic Revival style of the 1870s, you move down a flight to the Burgundy Room, which recreates the Edwardian Period. The main floor bar typifies an early-American saloon, with much of the woodwork made of African mahogany. Descending below ground level is Creighton's Emporium, complete with the actual wall from behind the prescription counter of the 1900 Old Town Drugstore.

Back upstairs in the Saloon I had their highly touted Strawberry Salad, which comes by its fame honestly, followed by a delicious taste of Brunswick Stew. Most of their recipes were found in an antique Virginia cookbook, but I believe their Quesadilla for vegetarians is an adapted creation. With my love for Mexican food, this dish gained high approval.

Naturally, their proximity to the ocean provides some marvelous seafood entrées, and my taste of their Backfin Crab Cake knows few parallels. When it comes to desserts, their Very Respectable Hot Fudge Sundae could add some very unrespectable pounds.

If extra poundage is a concern, then stay with their Onion Soup Fondue, a green salad and fresh strawberries for dessert.

Because my taste buds were experiencing a renaissance, I ordered Chateau Saint Michelle, a very smooth wine from Washington state.

Portner's is located at 109 Saint Asaph Street in Alexandria. Meals are served daily. Lunch is from 11:30 a.m.; dinner is from 6:00 p.m. until 10:30 p.m. weekdays, and one hour later on weekends. Sunday brunch is from 10:30 a.m. until 3:30 p.m. For reservations (recommended) call (703) 683-1776.

PORTNER'S STRAWBERRY SALAD

1 pint strawberries	ground black pepper
3 to 4 cucumbers	sprinkles of sugar
cabbage or Chinese celery	

Vinaigrette:

2 cups warm water	½ teaspoon salt
2 cups white vinegar	½ tablespoon coarsely
¾ cup sugar	ground pepper

Wash, destem and slice ripe strawberries in half and refrigerate. Peel cucumbers, slice lengthwise and scoop out seeds. Slice cucumbers ¼-inch thick in the shape of half moons. Combine ingredients for vinaigrette and marinate cucumbers for two hours in refrigerator.

To assemble salad, line chilled plates with the inner, tender leaves of cabbage or Chinese celery. Place a spoonful of marinated cucumbers on top of the cabbage leaves, and top with strawberries. Sprinkle additional cucumbers vinaigrette over berries. Top with freshly ground black pepper and a sprinkle of sugar. Serves 4 to 6.

PORTNER'S QUESADILLA

4 10-inch stone ground flour tortillas

1 cup grated Monterey Jack cheese

1 cup grated Colby cheese

2 ripe avocados

1 4¼-ounce can chili peppers, whole

1 cup Salsa Cilentro (recipe follows)

2 teaspoons crushed red peppers

3 tablespoons clarified butter or vegetable oil

2 ounces sour cream

Sprinkle tortillas evenly with both cheeses. Slice avocados thinly, and place slices over cheeses. Halve chili peppers; place over avocados. Spread salsa over peppers (reserving 4 teaspoons or so for garnish). Sprinkle with crushed red peppers. (Tortillas can be made ahead and refrigerated until needed.)

Pour clarified butter or oil into two 12-inch sauté pans (prepare tortillas one at a time). Cook tortillas over moderate heat until the cheese begins to melt and the bottom of the tortilla is lightly browned. Remove from pans and fold tortillas in half and place in casserole dish. Can be kept in 140-degree oven up to 45 minutes. Before serving, spoon sour cream and the extra salsa over tortillas. Serves 4.

Salsa Cilentro:

6 tomatoes, cored

2 to 3 fresh jalapeño peppers, cored

2 medium red onions, minced

1 teaspoon cumin

1 bunch fresh cilentro, stemmed (or 1 to 2 teaspoons of dried cilentro)

1½ teaspoons sugar

¾ teaspoon salt

Coarsely chop tomatoes and jalapeños and set aside. In food processor or blender, process remaining ingredients until mixture resembles a fine relish. Mix all ingredients together and store in tightly covered container in refrigerator until needed. Will keep for several days. Serves 4.

KENMORE INN
Fredericksburg

KENMORE INN

As my daughter and I walked up the path to the Kenmore Inn, its grand image set the scene for the soft, understated atmosphere of luxury that characterizes the inn's interior.

Although the inn, built as a private home in the late 1700s, has changed its status a number of times in the intervening years, we were lucky to discover it just one week after it had been completely renovated.

The renovation was done by the three proprietors, Dorothy Sampson and Maureen and Randolph Anderson. The Andersons are an English couple who have adopted Virginia because it reminds them of England.

Mrs. Anderson told us the interior required a major face-lift, but they were fortunate in utilizing the skills of her designer husband. Being very careful to maintain the fancy "egg and ball" carved woodwork used in the archways, Anderson has given the inn a unique blend of English and old Fredericksburg elegance.

The very wide, ornate foyer leads into either the bar, done in navy blue with petit point occasional chairs, or the main dining room, decorated in gray and pink pastels.

The main dining room was our selection for what I am told is a typical English lunch. Our table was set with a pink linen tablecloth and wine-colored napkins, and the forks were placed in the English manner, upside down. Fresh pink carnations and a sprig of lavender adorned our table.

A light salad garnished with fresh sprouts and the restaurant's own blend of hot tea began our meal. As recommended, I had their Scotch Pie, which is a good, hearty dish, but I also took some bites of Daintry's English Sausage Roll. It is a spicy sausage wrapped in puff pastry and served with Chutney Sauce.

For dessert I taste-tested the Eyemouth Tart, which reminds me of our Christmas fruit cakes, and a Cream Scone topped with black currant jelly.

We were not interested in alcoholic beverages at lunch, but the inn offers quite a nice selection.

The next time we visit Fredericksburg, it would be fun to stay in this posh English inn and be, as Mrs. Anderson suggests, "spoiled in the British manner."

The Kenmore Inn is located at 1200 Princess Anne Street in Fredericksburg. Lunch is served daily from 11:30 a.m. until 2:30 p.m. For reservations (recommended) call (703) 371-7622.

KENMORE INN'S RICH CREAM SCONES

1 cup plus 2 tablespoons plain flour	pinch of salt
1 tablespoon baking powder	4 to 5 tablespoons butter
	¼ cup sour cream
	1 egg

Sift flour and baking powder in bowl. Add salt, rub in butter lightly with fingertips. With a spoon make a deep hollow impression and pour in sour cream and well-beaten egg. Make into soft dough, turn onto floured board. Roll out lightly to ½-inch thickness. Cut into rounds, place on greased cookie sheet. Prick rounds with fork. Bake 10 to 12 minutes in 375-degree oven until golden. Serve with any jam or jelly. Yields 10 to 12.

KENMORE INN'S EYEMOUTH TART

8 ounces Pie Crust Pastry (see Index)	2 ounces cherries
6 tablespoons sugar	2 ounces raisins
2 ounces walnuts	1 egg, beaten
2 ounces currants	2 tablespoons butter, melted
2 ounces coconut, shredded	1 cup confectioners' sugar
	cold water

Roll out pastry and line 12-inch by 14-inch pan. Mix all dry ingredients, except confectioners' sugar. Add egg and melted butter and combine mixture. Spread mixture over pastry and bake in 375-degree oven until golden—about 30 minutes. Mix confectioners' sugar with enough cold water for spreading consistency. Ice while still hot. Yields 16.

KENMORE INN'S CUCUMBER CREAM FLAN

Pastry Dough:

5 ounces flour
dash of salt
6 tablespoons butter, cut in
  lumps

3 to 4 tablespoons iced
  water

In mixing bowl combine flour and salt; cut in butter lumps until grainy. Add iced water and press against bowl until it forms a mass. Remove and roll out on floured board and place in 7½-inch flan tin or 8-inch pie plate.

Flan:

2 cucumbers, sliced
4 ounces cream cheese
3 tablespoons mayonnaise
2 tablespoons chopped
  chives

salt and pepper to taste
cucumber slices for garnish

Finely chop cucumbers, except for garnish slices. Work cream cheese and mayonnaise in bowl until blended. Fold in cucumbers and chives. Salt and pepper to taste. Fill flan tin with mixture and level off with knife. Bake at 350 degrees about 25 to 30 minutes, until flan puffs up. Serves 6.

LA PETITE AUBERGE
Fredericksburg

LA PETITE AUBERGE The ladies who crossed the street in 1880 to prevent being seen walking past Mc-Cracken's, a liquor store with a questionable reputation, would be the first to walk through the door today.

A posh establishment known as La Petite Auberge has moved into this old store that has turned from liquor to hardware to excellent French cuisine.

The interior is really a surprise. Instead of a dark décor and the classical sounds of Vivaldi, it appears as a French sidewalk café, and the accompaniment is light, contemporary music. White latticed fences line exposed brick walls attractively decorated with paintings evocative of the French Impressionists. Tables are set with white linen, candles and fresh flowers.

After a day of traveling, a Strawberry Daiquiri was most tantalizing.

All the appetizers looked interesting, but since I had never tasted Asperges Ravigotte, I thought this was a good time. The presentation, which always adds so much to the enjoyment of a dish, was especially attractive. Strawberries and asparagus were cut into petals to form the shape of an unfolding flower.

My daughter, Daintry, was impressed, but pointed out that her Vichyssoise, garnished with strawberry slivers, was also something special.

I had been told by friends that I hadn't tasted Soft-shelled Crab until I'd tasted those at the Auberge. Prepared in an understated French sauce and garnished with almonds, this delicacy comes awfully close to a divine creation in my repertoire of food tasting. I decided on a 1975 Chateau La Gravette Bordeau to complement my seafood.

Daintry, who had Tornedoes au Poivre Vert, a beef tenderloin sautéed with green peppercorns, kept nudging me to get that recipe. But you can't get them all, and after trying their Sausage Casserole, I knew my husband would love that one. And he did.

For dessert, Daintry "pigged out" on their Grand Marnier Cake, while I sipped a French brandy.

On Wednesday night their lounge hosts different jazz groups, so drop by for a set. But you don't have to wait for Wednesday. The Auberge is a restaurant for any occasion.

La Petite Auberge is located at 311 William Street in Fredericksburg. Lunch is served Monday through Friday from 11:30 a.m. until 2:30 p.m. Dinner is served from 5:30 p.m. until 10:00 p.m., Monday through Saturday. The restaurant is closed the first Monday of each month. For reservations (required) call (703) 371-2727.

LA PETITE AUBERGE'S BACKFIN CRAB NORFOLK

5 tablespoons butter
1 teaspoon shallots,
  chopped
5 drops Tabasco sauce
1½ tablespoons capers
¼ teaspoon Old Bay
  Seasoning

1 pound backfin crabmeat
8 to 10 boiled new potatoes
lemon wedges
parsley for garnish

Melt butter to the foam stage, add shallots, Tabasco, capers and Old Bay Seasoning and cook until shallots are tender. Add crabmeat, swirl in skillet a few times, reduce heat to medium, cover and cook about 4 minutes. Serve with potatoes and garnish with lemon wedge and parsley. Serves 4.

LA PETITE AUBERGE'S SOFT-SHELLED CRABS

8 small soft-shelled crabs,
  cleaned
flour for dredging
4 tablespoons butter

salt and pepper to taste
2 ounces toasted almonds
2 shallots, chopped
1 lemon

Preheat oven to 450 degrees. Dredge soft-shelled crabs in flour. Using 2 skillets, melt 2 tablespoons of butter in each. Place 4 crabs in each skillet, back side down, for 2 to 3 minutes; turn over for 1 to 2 minutes. Salt and pepper to taste. Place both skillets in oven for 4 to 5 minutes with almonds, shallots and a squeeze of lemon juice over each. Serves 4.

LA PETITE AUBERGE'S BAKED SAUSAGE

2 pounds rope sausage
  (mild Italian)
2 green peppers, coarsely
  cut
1 red pepper, coarsely cut
3 small tomatoes, chopped
4 cloves garlic, crushed
½ teaspoon rosemary

½ teaspoon thyme
2 bay leaves
dash of crushed red pepper
¼ teaspoon fennel seeds
1 teaspoon cornstarch
1 cup dry white wine
fettucine (follow package
  directions)

Cut sausage into 12 equal portions. In mixing bowl, combine peppers, tomatoes, garlic, rosemary, thyme, bay leaves, crushed red pepper, fennel and cornstarch and stir until well mixed. Put mixture in bottom of large frying pan, placing sausage on top. Add wine and cook on top of stove until mixture reaches a boil; boil for about 3 minutes. Remove and bake in 425-degree oven, covered, for 25 to 30 minutes. Remove and serve with prepared fettucine. Serves 6 to 8.

OLDE MUDD TAVERN
Thornburg

OLDE MUDD TAVERN

All lines of communication were mysteriously down in Washington for over twenty-four hours following President Lincoln's assassination. During this time, injured assassin John Wilkes Booth made his way to Dr. Mudd in Thornburg.

Later, Booth's incriminating boot was found, unconcealed, in the doctor's office/home where he had set Booth's leg.

An angry investigation followed, and Mudd was accused of being an accomplice. Disregarding his former aid to Jackson in 1863 and to Longstreet and Lee before the Battle of Fredericksburg, the court sent Mudd to prison for treason.

He was later released but not cleared. Hence, the origin of the derogatory epithet "your name is mud."

It was not until 1979 that Dr. Mudd was exonerated, making the descendants of the entire Mudd family, which includes newsman Roger Mudd, relieved and happy.

Happy indeed is the atmosphere at the home of Dr. Mudd, now one of Virginia's most superb restaurants. As I entered the pre-Civil War home, the classical baroque sounds of a harpsichord, played in the foyer, began to push back the years for me.

I dined in the General Lee Room beneath Lee's portrait. Spring was in strong evidence at my table, appealingly set with a bouquet of irises and azaleas atop a linen tablecloth.

I realized this was going to be a one-of-a-kind feast when no less than five different freshly baked hot breads were served with apple butter. These gastronomical pleasures were followed by a relish tray and a wine list printed on a silver-colored fan.

A white chardonnay seemed an appropriate selection to enhance their Clam Appetizer and Deviled Crab Entrée. Both dishes are worth at least four stars, but their vegetables tip the five-star category. Zucchini in Tomato Sauce, Hawaiian Carrots, Creamed Spinach and Bourbon Sweet Potatoes are a ticket to culinary fame for owner and chef Vitarius.

Believe it or not, room was found for their Almond Cheesecake, which deserves not a star less than the other dishes.

Vitarius is equally creative in preparing dishes that won't ruin your calorie count. Prime Rib or Broiled Sirloin with a green salad should help you retain your status quo.

Wandering through the other dining rooms, also named for Southern generals, it was obvious that the sentiment remains in the South, but the cuisine belongs to no particular region. This restaurant is a true traveler's "find," which I intend to find again on my next trip.

The Olde Mudd Tavern is located on U.S. 1 and Route 606 in Thornburg. Meals are served Wednesday through Saturday, from 11:00 a.m. until 9:00 p.m., and from noon until 8:00 p.m. on Sunday. For reservations (recommended) call (703) 582-5250.

OLDE MUDD TAVERN'S
BOURBON SWEET POTATOES

½ pound brown sugar
1 46-ounce can of apple
  juice
2 cinnamon sticks
1 cup dark corn syrup

2 tablespoons cornstarch
½ cup water
1 ounce bourbon
1 pound sweet potatoes,
  boiled

In saucepan combine sugar, apple juice, cinnamon sticks and corn syrup over medium heat. Lower to simmer and cook one hour or more. Combine cornstarch with water and add to thicken mixture. Add bourbon, stirring to combine. Add boiled sweet potatoes and cook 20 minutes. Serves 4 to 6.

OLDE MUDD TAVERN'S ZUCCHINI
IN TOMATO SAUCE

Sauce:
1 small onion, chopped
2 stalks celery, chopped
½ of green pepper, chopped
½ cup fresh mushrooms,
  sliced
2 tablespoons oil

pinch of parsley
¼ teaspoon oregano
½ teaspoon garlic salt
pinch of sweet basil
1 16-ounce can of tomatoes
3 ounces tomato paste

In skillet, sauté vegetables in oil; add spices, tomatoes and tomato paste. Simmer for 1 hour.

Zucchini:

2 large zucchini　　　　　　**salt to taste**
3 tablespoons oil　　　　　　**pinch of oregano**
2 grinds of black pepper

Wash zucchini and rub down to smooth edges on peeling. Slice diagonally. In skillet, sauté in oil adding pepper, salt and oregano. Simmer until half-cooked and add sauce, cooking for 20 minutes. Serves 4 to 6.

OLDE MUDD TAVERN'S CREAMED SPINACH

Sauce:

6 to 8 bacon strips　　　　　**3 cups chicken stock**
1 small onion, chopped　　　**pinch of nutmeg**
1 to 2 teaspoons oil　　　　**salt and pepper to taste**
2 tablespoons flour　　　　　**2 tablespoons sour cream**

Fry bacon and set aside. Sauté onion in bacon drippings and drain grease. Add oil and flour, stirring to make a roux. Add chicken stock, stirring with whisk until slightly thickened to light sauce. Cook on medium-low heat about 30 minutes. Stir in nutmeg, and salt and pepper to taste. Add sour cream and heat through.

Spinach:

1 pound spinach　　　　　　**grind of black pepper**
2 tablespoons clarified　　　**salt to taste**
　butter　　　　　　　　　　**2 ounces anisette**

Wash spinach well and remove stems. Dip spinach in boiling water until it wilts. Remove, drain, and set aside to cool. In skillet, add butter and cooled spinach; add a grind of pepper and salt, sautéing for 5 minutes. Add anisette and simmer 5 minutes. Add sauce and simmer until flavors blend for 20 to 30 minutes. Serves 4 to 6.

FOX HEAD INN
Manakin-Sabot

FOX HEAD INN

The TV cameras were rolling, and the director shouted, "Action!" Then the stuntman for popular daytime soap *Search For Tomorrow* walked forward as, on cue, the car spun in the Fox Head Inn's driveway, "hit" its intended victim, and sped away from the scene of the crime.

On the soap, the inn is called The Hartford House. Fox Head was chosen for filming because its pastoral beauty and authentic nineteenth-century architectural charm produced just the right setting.

Fox Head's manager, Scott Pettit, made what he called his television debut and exit when he held an IV over the actor who was supposedly being rushed to the hospital.

Scott's mother, Barbara Pettit, told me they hadn't had so much excitement in this tucked-away corner of historic Goochland County since the evening an avalanche of secret service men tumbled out of two black limousines. They had come to check the security for a Saudi Arabian sheik. The sheik was visiting the area to study a local hospital and was advised, excellently so, to dine at the Fox Head.

The restaurant is described as a farmhouse. It was built at the turn of the century by Mr. Raleigh Mills. It's been said that Mills had to raise the original one-story roof with railroad jacks in order to provide additional room for his seven children. Perhaps it's the height that gives the structure a more elegant appearance than the usual farmhouse.

Inside, the four dining rooms depict past and present regional interests. The Hunt Room conveys the restaurant's name and is decorated in the pinks of fox hunters. It features an unusual horseshoe-shaped table and various hunting paraphernalia. The Country Kitchen is adorned with old bottles and the now rare, blue graniteware. The Thoroughbred Room displays not only the pictures of winning horses from local stables but also miniature jockey figurines, mounted on wall brackets, wearing their stables' colors.

It would be difficult to choose a favorite, but I am partial to the Tobacco Room. My daughter, Daintry, and I dined in this nostalgic room that sports a gigantic old Bull Durham poster, the type I used to see on highway billboards when I was a child.

Daintry was especially pleased with their Seafood Casserole—a combination of shrimp and lobster in a sherry-cream sauce. I decided on the Scampi, cooked with Dijon mustard and lemon juice in a white wine sauce. The beauty of this dish is it doesn't taste low-cal, but it is!

The Fox Head's cuisine, which also includes steaks and fried chicken, was described in *Victorian Magazine* as "neither haute cuisine, nor city slick, nor country." It is, however, excellent, with especially creative touches given to vegetables, in particular the Cymling (squash) Cakes, and desserts.

Two of their real standout desserts are the Fox Hunter Pie, served with a bourbon-laced, whipped cream topping, and their homemade Creme de Menthe Ice Cream.

The Midori cocktails we imbibed before dinner and the Virginia wine ordered with dinner helped make dining at the Fox Head a relaxing and memorable experience.

The Fox Head Inn is located on Route 621 in Manakin-Sabot. Dinner is served Monday through Saturday from 6:30 p.m. For reservations (required) call (804) 784-5126.

FOX HEAD INN'S CYMLING CAKES

1 large cymling (squash)
1 medium Vidalia onion, grated
1 egg, beaten
½ teaspoon salt
1 tablespoon sugar

1 cup flour
1½ teaspoons baking powder
¼ teaspoon pepper
oil for frying

Grate squash, using coarse side of grater. In medium-sized mixing bowl, place grated cymling and grated onions, and add all ingredients except oil. Mix until thoroughly incorporated. Shape mixture into 8 patties. Pour about 2 tablespoons of oil into skillet and fry patties on both sides over medium-high heat until cooked through the centers. Serves 4.

FOX HEAD INN'S BLUE CHEESE DRESSING

1 pint mayonnaise
¾ cup buttermilk
¼ teaspoon garlic powder
½ teaspoon Worcestershire
  sauce

2 tablespoons crushed
  pineapple
2 ounces blue cheese,
  crumbled

In blender or mixing bowl, add mayonnaise and buttermilk and blend until mixed. Add garlic powder, Worcestershire sauce and crushed pineapple and mix until smooth. Add blue cheese and mix only until combined. Pour in container with tight fitting lid and store in refrigerator. Yields over 3 cups.

THE TOBACCO COMPANY
RESTAURANT
Richmond

THE TOBACCO COMPANY

A first-time excursion to The Tobacco Company is tantamount to a saucy flirtation with Southern history. Passing an ancient wooden Indian on the main floor, you immediately experience the triple-tier effect of an atrium reaching all the way to the skylight roof on the third floor. Visually stunning, this architectural feat bathes each floor with an airy lightness that embellishes the regal austerity of the restaurant's Victorian antiques.

Before dining in this 1878 tobacco warehouse, take the scenic tour. You can either climb the recycled stairway from Richmond's Saint Luke's Hospital or make your ascent in the brass elevator. Arriving on the top floor, a greenhouse solarium decorated with white wicker renders the feeling that you are picnicking in an old Southern garden. The second floor offers little offices for private dining. I was lucky to get a table by the balcony, affording me a panoramic view of the restaurant and its twelve-foot brass chandelier that hangs from the skylight.

Because my weight scale was on tilt, I ordered their Pasta Light-Line Salad, available only at lunch. This salad is as filling as it is tasty. Somewhere between my salad and their savory Mary Martin's Low-Calorie Cheese Pie (also offered only at lunch), their "sheik story" was unraveled for me.

One day the restaurant received a call from a man who identified himself as a State Department official. He told them to expect an Arab oil tycoon for dinner. Hours later, the press began to camp out as "security personnel" came to check out the kitchen. Finally, a man attired in an Arab costume, complete with sunglasses, arrived in a Rolls Royce. His "Exxon security," plus a phalanx of news photographers, surrounded his entourage as they were shuttled to a private dining area. That evening the sheik dined in the style of a tycoon, and in tune with Arabic convention, did not speak. As it turned out, he was not a sheik, but a Roanoke school teacher whose friends had aided him in accomplishing this elaborate hoax.

While dining as a sheik, I wondered if the teacher had ordered the Veal Piccata, which is, to my taste buds, a royal offering. The staff doesn't remember his entrée, but they do recall that a number of fine wines were consumed.

The next time I'm in Richmond I plan to spend some time in their nightclub below the main level. It features a disc jockey, dancing and hors d'oeuvres. But of course I'll take another tour upstairs because a single visit isn't sufficient to take in all the memorabilia that imparts this restaurant's romance with the past.

The Tobacco Company Restaurant is located at 1201 East Cary Street in Richmond's Shockoe Slip. Lunch is served from 11:30 a.m. until 2:30 p.m. and dinner is from 5:30 p.m. until 10:30 p.m., Monday through Friday. Dinner is served on Saturday from 5:00 p.m. until midnight. On Sunday, brunch is served from 10:30 a.m. until 2:00 p.m., and dinner is from 5:30 p.m. until 10:00 p.m. The Tobacco Company Club is open from 8:00 p.m. until 2:00 a.m., Monday through Saturday. Reservations are accepted for the first hour of service only. Call (804) 643-6560.

THE TOBACCO COMPANY RESTAURANT'S PASTA LIGHT-LINE SALAD

3 quarts water
1 tablespoon salt
1 teaspoon salad oil
8 ounces seashell pasta
1 large zucchini, peeled and
  sliced
½ bunch broccoli
  flowerettes
2 carrots, sliced
1 egg

4 radish roses
2 cups spinach, stemmed
  and steamed
½ cup herb dressing (from
  your grocery)
1 tomato, sliced
4 tablespoons Parmesan
  cheese
20 black pitted olives

Bring water, salt and salad oil to a boil in a large pot. Gradually add pasta and continue to boil, uncovered, until pasta is tender (about 15 minutes). Drain, rinse with cold water, and chill. Steam zucchini, broccoli and carrots approximately 2 to 3 minutes. Boil an egg. Make radish roses. Toss pasta with cleaned and chilled spinach, steamed and cooled vegetables and herb dressing. Garnish with tomatoes, radishes, egg slices, Parmesan cheese and black olives. Serves 4 to 6.

THE TOBACCO COMPANY RESTAURANT'S
VEAL PICCATA

flour for veal
4 2- to 3-ounce veal cutlets,
  thinly sliced and
  pounded flat
1 egg, beaten
½ cup bread crumbs
½ cup Romano cheese

2 tablespoons butter
juice of 1 lemon
½ cup mushrooms, sliced
4 tablespoons red wine
1 cup Demi-Glace (recipe
  follows)

Lightly flour veal and dip in an egg wash; dip veal in bread crumbs and Romano cheese. Sauté in butter until each side has browned. Splash veal with lemon juice and remove from pan. Add the mushrooms to pan and sauté briefly. Add wine and Demi-Glace. Simmer to reduce slightly. Pour sauce over veal. Serves 4.

Demi-Glace:
1 cup brown sauce
1 cup beef stock

½ cup Marsala wine

Combine brown sauce, beef stock and Marsala wine. Mix well.

SAM MILLER'S WAREHOUSE
Richmond

SAM MILLER'S WAREHOUSE

What is the difference between pornographic nudity and artistic nudity, and how in the world does either relate to Shockoe Slip's oldest restaurant? The former proprietors of this one-hundred-year-old restaurant did have to clarify the difference for the ABC Board or be closed down. The dilemma arose over two famous nude prints displayed behind the bar. I am happy to say that art won. The nudes, *September Morn* and Goya's controversial masterpiece of his duchess, *Nude Maja*, came close to being viewed by museum-goers only.

Because Sam Miller's Warehouse restaurant transmits a sort of rustic, casual mood, it has become a comfortable place for the younger crowd to hang out. Nobody feels they have to get dressed up for this former meat and poultry warehouse.

Another reason the Warehouse has become a favorite is that the food is as unpretentious as the décor. The restaurant has developed a reputation for specialty soups and sandwiches. My favorite is the Cheese Cauliflower Soup. It's not exactly a diet concoction, but as my grandmother would say, "It'll stick to your ribs." If you already have too much sticking to your ribs, then order the Spinach Salad or their Mushroom Quiche.

Most people come for dinner because they are ready to "chow down" on a large Beef Fillet or Oysters Three Ways. Others come for the two-for-one happy hour and the after-dinner rock and roll lounge that features the latest rock groups in the area.

There is, as you may have guessed, a wide assortment of alcoholic offerings. The often overheard saying at the Warehouse is: "When you see the moose wearing the chef's hat on the wall wink at you, then you know it's time to get someone else to drive home."

Sam Miller's Warehouse restaurant is located at 1210 East Cary Street in Richmond's Shockoe Slip. Food is served from

11:00 a.m. until 11:00 p.m., Sunday through Thursday, and from 11:00 a.m. until 1:00 a.m. on Friday and Saturday. For reservations (recommended) call (804) 643-1301.

WAREHOUSE'S OYSTERS THREE WAYS

Bienville:

2 teaspoons fresh, sliced mushrooms	1 tablespoon olive oil
2 teaspoons fresh, chopped parsley	⅓ cup diced, tiny shrimp
1½ tablespoons chopped scallions	3 ounces backfin crabmeat
	12 oysters, shucked

Sauté mushrooms, parsley and scallions in oil; add shrimp, sautéing lightly; fold in crabmeat and heat through. Remove and set aside to cool.

Sauce:

1 slice bacon	1 tablespoon plus 1 teaspoon lemon juice
½ clove of garlic, minced	1 tablespoon plus 1 teaspoon sherry
½ stick of butter	
3 heaping tablespoons flour	
1 cup heated milk	

In skillet, fry bacon and cook garlic in bacon drippings. Remove bacon from skillet, drain. Melt butter in skillet, stirring in flour to make a roux. When sauce reaches smooth consistency, slowly add heated milk, stirring to incorporate. Return bacon to skillet, add lemon juice and sherry, heating through. Place shrimp and crabmeat mixture on four separate plates and add 3 raw oysters to each; cover with sauce.

Rockefeller:

¼ stick butter, melted	dash of white pepper
1 small onion, chopped	6 cups fresh spinach
½ small bay leaf, crushed	1 teaspoon Pernod
1 tablespoon fresh parsley	¼ cup bread crumbs
½ teaspoon celery seed	¼ cup Parmesan cheese
dash of salt	12 oysters
dash of Tabasco sauce	

Melt butter in saucepan and sauté onion, bay leaf, parsley and celery seed. Add dashes of salt, Tabasco sauce and white pepper. Cook spinach leaves in boiling water until wilted. Drain spinach and add sautéed seasonings, Pernod, bread crumbs and Parmesan cheese, heating through. Place 3 raw oysters on each plate and cover with spinach mixture.

Casino Butter:

1 stick butter	2 teaspoons lemon juice
½ clove of garlic, minced	dash of Worcestershire
3 tablespoons chopped	sauce
parsley	12 oysters

Soften butter and cream together with garlic, parsley, lemon juice and Worcestershire sauce until well combined. Place 3 oysters on each plate and cover with butter mixture. Place all three oyster combinations under broiler for about one minute. Use tin, steel or oven-proof plates for this dish. Serves 4.

WAREHOUSE'S CHEESE CAULIFLOWER SOUP

1 large head of cauliflower	6 ounces American cheese
1 teaspoon salt	1 stick butter
2½ cups flour	salt and pepper to taste
1½ quarts milk	

Break up cauliflower into flowerettes and put in boiling, salted water. Lower heat and cook until almost tender. In separate, unheated large pot, put flour and add 1 quart of milk, gradually working to smooth consistency. In another saucepan, melt cheese and butter together. Turn heat to medium low under milk and flour mixture, stirring constantly as cheese mixture is added. Drain cauliflower and add to mixture. Heat through. If mixture is too thick, slowly add half a quart of milk. Salt and pepper to taste. Serves 8 to 10.

HANOVER TAVERN
Hanover

HANOVER TAVERN

Few people know that, while earning his law degree, Patrick Henry tended bar (often barefoot) at Hanover Tavern. His alternative occupation was the result of marriage to Sarah, the daughter of tavern owner John Shelton. The young couple lived at the tavern that was originally built as a stagecoach stop in 1723. And, it was from the tavern that Henry was called across the street to the courthouse in 1763 to fight for the farmers against King George III. Henry's case, ironically known as the Parsons' Cause, was actually anti-parsons. Henry proved that parsons were the guilty middlemen in a royal tax "rip-off" of the colonial farmers.

History had yet other episodes to record at the Hanover, and some eighteen years later, word came to the tavern that Cornwallis and Tarleton were approaching. Remember those old western movies in which everyone ran out of the saloon and jumped on the first available horse? It is said that when the British were sighted, the exit was so hasty that it took a week before all the horses were returned to their rightful owners. During this confusion, Cornwallis requisitioned the tavern and made it his headquarters for eighteen days, and then left—neglecting to pay his bill.

The bill of fare in these colonial dining rooms varies with each theatrical production at the adjacent Barksdale Theatre. The night of our visit we enjoyed Ham Biscuits, their famous Stewed Apples, Shrimp Salad and Cheese Corn—all washed down with a light rosé wine. The custard-type cake looked very appetizing, but my calorie counter told me that I'd better substitute the play for dessert. And what a dessert it was. *A Coupla White Chicks Sitting Around Talking* surely aided my calorie reduction because I expended so much energy laughing!

It's good entertainment, which is what this oldest dinner theater in America is famous for. The repertoire includes everything from *Antigone* to musicals, with a sprinkling of light opera. The Barksdale Theatre group, which began renovating this tavern in 1953, has converted it into a living historical landmark. However, this establishment goes one step beyond by serving both delicious food and great theater. An unbeatable combination!

Hanover Tavern and Barksdale Theatre are located on Highway 301 in Hanover. Cocktails are served from 6:00 p.m.; dinner is served from 7:00 p.m. until 8:30 p.m., Wednesday through Saturday. Year-round performances, given Wednesday through Saturday, begin at 8:30 p.m. For reservations (required) call (804) 798-6547.

HANOVER TAVERN'S STEWED APPLES

2 cups apples, cooked and
   mashed
½ cup brown sugar
4 tablespoons cornstarch
1 teaspoon cinnamon

½ teaspoon nutmeg
1 teaspoon vanilla
1 teaspoon lemon juice
½ teaspoon salt
3 tablespoons butter

Place apples in medium-size bowl; mix sugar and cornstarch and add to apples, mixing well. Add remaining ingredients, except butter, and mix thoroughly. Pour mixture into an 8-inch square, greased baking dish and dot with butter. Bake in 350-degree oven for 30 to 45 minutes. Serves 6.

HANOVER TAVERN'S SHRIMP SALAD

1 pound tiny shrimp,
   shelled and boiled
1 pound macaroni, cooked
½ cup grated cabbage
⅓ cup mayonnaise
⅓ cup pickle relish

1½ tablespoons mustard
1 teaspoon celery seed
1 celery stalk, diced
2 tablespoons onion, grated
1 egg, hard boiled, chopped

In large mixing bowl, combine all ingredients using mayonnaise to bind. May add more mayonnaise if necessary. Chill. Serves 8 to 10.

HANOVER TAVERN'S CHEESE CORN

1 16-ounce can of corn
5 tablespoons grated sharp
  Cheddar cheese
½ of small green pepper,
  chopped

½ of small onion, chopped
salt and pepper to taste
¾ stick butter
2 pieces cubed bread,
  toasted

In mixing bowl, place drained corn, cheese, green pepper, onion, salt and pepper, mixing well. In saucepan, melt butter and add cubed toast or bread crumbs. Pour corn mixture into an 8-inch, greased baking dish, and cover with butter and bread crumb mixture. Bake in 350-degree oven about 30 minutes or until golden brown. Serves 4.

HALF WAY HOUSE
Petersburg

HALF WAY HOUSE Yes, George Washington did
sleep here. So did Robert E.
Lee and Ulysses S. Grant
(thankfully, not at the same time). Built in 1760 on a land
grant from George II of England, the Half Way House, located halfway between Petersburg and Richmond, served as
a stagecoach stop and ordinary. An ordinary was a lodge that
assigned sleeping space according to a traveler's station in
life. The guests slept upstairs dormitory-style and ate downstairs in the Gentlemen's Tap Room. The kitchen was then,
as it is today, in a separate building just a stone's throw from
the dining room. In those days, the cooks were not only
expected to transport the food but also to whistle or sing in
the process. This supposedly prevented food from being
snitched along the way. Today, the food is still speedily trans-
ferred to your table, but the whistling has long since gone by
the boards.

To enter the dining room, you must walk down the original
brick steps, worn smooth from centuries of famous footsteps. Whether your footsteps add another famed note to
this dining room is of little consequence to the headwaiter,
James, who has been here for forty-two years. James greets
everyone with the graciousness that defines true Southern
hospitality.

A cool mist fell the evening I visited, giving the fireplaces
an extra dimension of welcome in this room that clearly re-
veres the simplicity of the past.

Seated beside a calico-curtained window, I had a glass of
Colonial Hot Spiced Wine, accompanied by exquisite little
Cinnamon Rolls—a tasty way to warm your bones. This was
followed by an excellent appetizer of homemade Vegetable
Soup. Their Filet Mignon, served with grapes and fried shrimp,
is delicious. I also sampled the Green Beans—so good I asked
for their recipe. I also recommend their colonial Gingerbread
with Hard Sauce for dessert.

The wine selection, like the atmosphere, is simple but excellent. As I sat enjoying a glass of after-dinner wine, I felt

that I had moved back to a time when moments were savored like slow sips of wine.

The Half Way House is located at 10301 Jefferson Davis Highway between Petersburg and Richmond. Dinner is served daily from 5:30 p.m. until 10:00 p.m. For reservations (recommended) call (804) 275-1760.

HALF WAY HOUSE'S HOT SPICED WINE

1 quart dry red wine
1 cup water
1 cup sugar
1 teaspoon whole cloves
1 cinnamon stick
1 lemon, sliced
½ of orange, sliced

Combine all ingredients in a large pot. Bring to boil over high heat, then simmer for 15 minutes. Strain and serve hot. Serves 10.

HALF WAY HOUSE'S GREEN BEANS

6 strips bacon
1 medium onion, finely
  chopped
4 tomatoes, chopped
2 tablespoons sugar
salt and pepper to taste
2 16-ounce cans of French-
  style green beans

Fry bacon until crisp. Fry onions in bacon grease until light brown. Add tomatoes, sugar, salt and pepper. Simmer until tomatoes are soft. Add beans and continue to simmer until heated through. Crumble bacon and add just before serving. Serves 8 to 10.

HALF WAY HOUSE'S FRENCH DRESSING

1 cup cider vinegar
2 teaspoons paprika
½ tablespoon dry, ground
   mustard

2 teaspoons sugar
1 garlic clove, minced
1 cup cotton seed oil
¼ onion, quartered

Mix vinegar, paprika, mustard, sugar and garlic until thoroughly incorporated. Add oil and blend in blender. Add onion to dressing and allow to set overnight in refrigerator. Remove onion and serve. Yields 2 cups.

CHOWNING'S TAVERN
Williamsburg

CHOWNING'S TAVERN

Spreading the loosely woven napkin in my lap reminded me of how long it took our colonial ancestors to weave just one small square of fabric. And, for that matter, how long it took them to prepare one meal. Yet, even without our modern shortcuts, they did reserve time for enjoying themselves, even the common folk.

Chowning's catered to the tastes of the working man with grogs and ales served then, as they are today, in blue and white salt-glazed mugs. The food was most likely fresh fish and game heaped on pewter plates.

The current waiters, mostly William and Mary students, are dressed in red knee breeches, but I'll bet in 1766 when Josiah Chowning opened the doors of his tavern, the servants were more simply attired. Today's reconstructed building and interior furnishings of sturdy wood tables and chairs are not, however, unlike those that Chowning would have provided for his patrons. Even the cartoons on the walls attest to the merrymaking that goes on after nine o'clock when Chowning's becomes Gambols. The atmosphere reverts to an eighteenth-century tavern complete with magician. Guests are encouraged to enter into games of Goose and Loo that are played quite literally for peanuts.

I missed the evening entertainment, but thoroughly enjoyed having lunch upstairs beneath a dormer window. I had been told that their Welsh Rarebit is exceptional, and it is, but my favorite dish of all is the Black Walnut Ice Cream. I remembered that particular ice cream from several summers ago when I lunched outdoors under Chowning's grape arbor canopy. On that very hot day I strongly appreciated a Mint Julep from the bar and a light Chicken Salad Plate.

For the evening fare, the favored dish is Roast Prime Rib of Beef. Chowning's Good Bread and their garden salad with a special Chutney Dressing are popular, also. My suggestion to you would be to go late enough to stay and join in an eighteenth-century evening of fun and spirits when Chowning's changes into Gambols.

Chowning's Tavern is located on the Duke of Gloucester Street in Williamsburg. Lunch is served daily from 11:30 a.m. until 3:30 p.m., and dinner is served from 5:00 p.m. until 8:30 p.m. Gambols is open from 9:00 p.m. until 1:00 a.m. Winter hours may vary. For reservations (required for Chowning's but not accepted for Gambols) call (804) 229-2141.

CHOWNING'S TAVERN'S BLACK WALNUT ICE CREAM

8 egg yolks
1¼ cups sugar
dash of salt
2 cups milk
2 cups whipping cream

1 teaspoon black walnut extract
1 cup black walnuts, chopped

Beat the egg yolks with the sugar until creamy; add the salt. In a saucepan bring the milk and cream almost to boiling, but do not boil. Remove from heat and pour slowly into the egg mixture, stirring constantly. Add the black walnut extract. Heat to scalding. Pour the mixture into a one-gallon freezer container of an ice cream maker. Follow the manufacturer's instructions for freezing. When the dasher is removed, add the black walnuts, stirring to distribute them evenly. Pack as freezing instructions direct and allow to "ripen" at least 3 hours before serving. Yields 1½ quarts.

CHOWNING'S TAVERN'S WELSH RAREBIT

1 tablespoon butter
1 pound sharp Cheddar cheese, grated
¾ cup beer
dash of cayenne pepper (or Tabasco sauce)

1 teaspoon dry mustard
½ teaspoon salt
½ teaspoon Worcestershire sauce
1 egg, slightly beaten
1 teaspoon cornstarch

Melt butter in the top of a double boiler. Add the cheese and all but one tablespoon of beer. Cook over hot (but not boiling) water until the cheese melts. Combine the season-

175

ings with the remaining tablespoon of beer and the Worcestershire sauce, and stir into the cheese. Combine the slightly beaten egg with the cornstarch; stir into the cheese mixture and let it thicken slightly. Serve immediately over toast or broiled tomato halves. Serves 4.

CHOWNING'S TAVERN'S WINE COOLER

¾ cup lemonade   sprig of mint
¼ cup dry red wine   maraschino cherry

Pour the lemonade over crushed ice in 10-ounce tumbler, then add the red wine. Garnish with a sprig of mint and a cherry. Serves 1.

CHOWNING'S TAVERN'S BROWNIES

1 cup butter
8 ounces unsweetened
  chocolate
7 eggs
3 cups sugar
½ teaspoon vanilla

2 cups sifted all-purpose
  flour
1 tablespoon baking
  powder
2 cups pecans, chopped

Preheat the oven to 350 degrees. Grease a 10½-inch by 15½-inch by 1-inch pan. Melt the butter and chocolate in a double boiler over hot water. In mixing bowl beat the eggs, sugar and vanilla until frothy. Add the melted butter and chocolate. Add the sifted dry ingredients. Stir in the pecans. Pour into the prepared pan and bake at 350 degrees for 30 minutes. Cool and cut into 3-inch by 3-inch squares. Yields 20.

Note: The recipes from all the Williamsburg restaurants are used through the courtesy of *The Williamsburg Cookbook*. Each recipe was tested again for this book.

CHRISTIANA CAMPBELL'S TAVERN
Williamsburg

CHRISTIANA CAMPBELL'S TAVERN

Of all the taverns in Williamsburg, Christiana Campbell's 1771 hostelry, according to George Washington's diary, was his favorite. Whether he was lured by the food, the accommodations at this "good dwelling house" or the plump and bawdy Mrs. Campbell, known for her earthy tales and humor, history does not say; it only hints. I must say, though, that reading between the lines certainly casts a less austere profile on the age. They really had a good time, as I did the morning I brunched here.

The gambrel-roofed, colonial frame house has been faithfully reconstructed. Early records indicate a blue-gray décor, imitated today right down to the checked linen curtains and the original Lambeth delftware, reproduced for this restaurant only.

I'm always fascinated by obscure differences, and the sugar container on the wooden table caught my eye. A reproduction from the tavern's early days, it is called a "muffin ear" and pours from the center.

I began brunch with the very best Pecan Waffles I've ever tasted, along with a side order of tiny, Sweet Potato Muffins that won't let you stop with just one. Then, because I'd never tasted Fig Ice Cream, I sampled this very unusual dessert. Equally delicious was their Rum Cream Pie.

What a calorie binge! I could have had a much lighter meal with their version of the colonial Salmagundi (chef's salad) for lunch or their unique Shad Roe Omelet.

If you go for dinner you'll be entertained by strolling minstrels. Because the tavern focuses on seafood from the Chesapeake Bay, my dinner suggestion would be their popular A Made Dish of Shrimp and Lobster or the Deviled Backfin Crabmeat.

Although I rarely choose a mixed drink, their Black Velvet Cocktail, an elixir of champagne and Guinness Stout, does pose an intriguing invitation. But then, I found the entire personality of the tavern to be a warm invitation to another age.

Christiana Campbell's Tavern is located on Waller Street in Williamsburg. Brunch is served daily from 10:00 a.m. until 2:30 p.m., and dinner from 5:30 p.m. until 9:30 p.m. Winter hours may vary. For reservations (required for dinner) call (804) 229-2141.

CHRISTIANA CAMPBELL'S TAVERN'S
SWEET POTATO MUFFINS

⅔ cup canned or fresh
   cooked sweet potatoes,
   well drained
4 tablespoons butter
½ cup sugar
1 egg
¾ cup all-purpose flour
2 teaspoons baking powder

½ teaspoon salt
½ teaspoon cinnamon
¼ teaspoon nutmeg
½ cup milk
4 tablespoons pecans or
   walnuts, chopped
4 tablespoons raisins,
   chopped

Preheat oven to 400 degrees. Grease muffin tins that are 1½ inches in diameter. Purée the sweet potatoes in a food processor or blender. Cream the butter and sugar. Beat in the egg and puréed sweet potatoes. Sift the flour with the baking powder, salt, cinnamon and nutmeg. Add dry ingredients alternately by hand with the milk, chopped nuts and raisins, mixing just until blended. Do not overmix. Spoon into the greased muffin tins, filling each completely full. A little sugar and cinnamon may be sprinkled on top of each muffin, if desired. Bake at 400 degrees for 25 minutes. Yields 30 muffins.

CHRISTIANA CAMPBELL'S TAVERN'S
RUM CREAM PIE

1 envelope unflavored
   gelatin
½ cup cold water
5 egg yolks
1 cup sugar
⅓ cup dark rum

1½ cups whipping cream
1 9-inch graham cracker pie
   crust
unsweetened chocolate for
   garnish

Soften the gelatin in ½ cup of cold water. Place over low heat and bring almost to a boil, stirring to dissolve. Beat the egg yolks and sugar until very light. Stir the gelatin into the egg mixture; cool. Gradually add the rum, beating constantly. In separate bowl whip the cream until it stands in soft peaks and fold it into the gelatin mixture. Cool until the mixture begins to set, then spoon it into the crumb crust and chill until firm enough to cut. Grate the unsweetened chocolate over the top before serving. Yields 1 pie.

CHRISTIANA CAMPBELL'S TAVERN'S
A MADE DISH OF SHRIMP AND LOBSTER

1½ green peppers, quartered

3 medium tomatoes

1 6-ounce package long-grain rice

1 6-ounce package wild rice

½ pound fresh mushrooms, quartered

¼ pound butter, divided

¾ pound lobster, cooked and shelled

1 pound shrimp, cooked and cleaned

1 15½-ounce can pearl onions

¾ cup dry sherry

1 teaspoon lemon juice

Worcestershire sauce to taste

salt and white pepper to taste

parsley, chopped (optional)

Partially cook the green pepper in boiling water, remove from water and cut the quarters in half. Reserve. Scald tomatoes in boiling water for 60 seconds; drain, remove skin and cut in half. Squeeze out and discard tomato juice and seeds and cut each half into 4 pieces. Reserve. Mix the two kinds of rice and cook according to package instructions. Set aside. Sauté the mushrooms quickly in a small amount of butter and reserve. Cut the lobster into bite-sized pieces. Melt the remaining butter over medium heat and sauté the lobster, shrimp and onions. Add the sherry, lemon juice and seasonings. Add the green pepper, tomatoes and mushrooms and simmer over low heat, stirring gently, until heated through. Arrange the seafood and vegetables in a heated serving dish with rice. Garnish with chopped parsley if desired. Serves 4 to 6.

KING'S ARMS TAVERN
Williamsburg

KING'S ARMS TAVERN

Guests are probably more apt to notice the classical decorating that enhances the bright Williamsburg green fireplaces and moldings at the King's Arms rather than the obscure architectural feature of reversed balusters on the stairs. I was fascinated to find that the seventh and thirteenth balusters were purposely turned upside down. There are two theories. The first is that they were positioned in opposition to the others to ward off evil spirits; the second holds that colonial people purposely built in flaws to reaffirm their belief that only God was perfect.

Hence, when the tavern was replicated on its 1770 site, historically sensitive architects complied with the early colonial beliefs.

Historical research reveals that Jane Vobe operated the King's Arms, reputedly one of the most genteel taverns in the city. The Virginia aristocracy was fed with Travis House Oyster Pie, Colonial Game Pie, Cream of Peanut Soup and Sally Lunn Bread. These colonial dishes continue to serve such important guests as Queen Elizabeth, Theodore Hess and a former Secretary of State. A waiter, who served the Secretary, asked if he would like to have the bill sent to his home, to which the Secretary enthusiastically replied, "Yes, I would." The waiter then asked, "Your home address, sir?" The Secretary looked puzzled, turned to his wife and asked, "Where do we live?" Is it any wonder our foreign policy has problems?

The day I lunched at the tavern, I had no problem in choosing the refreshing Frosted Fruit Shrub and Chicken Pot Pie, one of their celebrated colonial dishes. To my pleasure, the pie had no resemblance to the frozen variety found in supermarkets. Had I wanted a lighter meal, I could have had their King's Arms Salad Bowl with strips of Smithfield ham, turkey, cheese and their house dressing. Instead, I went right to a dessert of Colonial Meringue with fresh strawberries— exactly the right light touch.

The tavern would be an excellent evening choice with its

good selection of fine wines and beers and strolling balladeers who perform with lutes and sing merry songs of colonial days.

The King's Arms Tavern is located on the Duke of Gloucester Street in Williamsburg. Lunch is served from 11:30 a.m. to 2:30 p.m., and dinner from 5:30 p.m. to 9:30 p.m. daily from April through December. Check on winter serving hours. For reservations (required) call (804) 229-2141.

KING'S ARMS TAVERN'S CHICKEN POT PIE

2 chickens (2½ to 3 pounds each)
2 ribs of celery, chopped
1 medium onion, sliced
1 bay leaf
1 teaspoon salt
½ teaspoon white pepper
½ cup butter
½ cup all-purpose flour
1 10-ounce package frozen peas, cooked
4 ribs celery, diced and cooked
4 carrots, sliced and cooked
1¾ cups potatoes, diced and cooked
1 egg
2 tablespoons milk
Pastry Crust (recipe below)

Preheat the oven to 375 degrees 10 minutes before the pies are to go in. Grease 8 individual casseroles. Put the chicken on to cook in a large pan with enough water to cover. Add 2 chopped ribs of celery, onion, bay leaf, salt and pepper. Bring the water to a boil, reduce the heat to simmer, and cook until the chicken is done. Remove the fat and strain the stock. Cut chicken into large pieces. In a saucepan melt the butter and stir in flour. Cook 5 minutes, stirring constantly. Add enough chicken stock, stirring constantly, to achieve a light and creamy consistency. Simmer 5 minutes. Add salt and pepper to taste. Divide the chicken and cooked vegetables equally into 8 individual casseroles. Add to each the amount of sauce desired, stirring the chicken and vegetables to mix thoroughly. Mix egg and milk together. Cover each casserole with pastry, brush with the egg mixture and puncture pastry with a fork to allow steam to escape. Bake at 375 degrees until crust is golden brown. Serves 8.

Pastry Crust:

3 cups all-purpose flour   **1 cup shortening**
1 teaspoon salt   **ice water**
2 teaspoons sugar

Mix the dry ingredients together. Blend in the shortening with knives or a pastry blender until the mixture is of pebbly consistency. Store in a covered container in refrigerator. When ready to use, moisten the pastry mix with enough ice water to hold the dough together and divide into 8 equal portions. Roll out on a lightly floured board.

KING'S ARMS TAVERN'S TENDERLOIN OF BEEF STUFFED WITH OYSTERS

4 7-ounce tenderloin steaks   **4 slices bacon**
12 medium oysters   **1 teaspoon parsley, chopped**
salt and pepper to taste   **(or fresh chives, snipped)**
3 tablespoons butter,
   divided

Insert a sharp knife into the side of each tenderloin steak and, with a short sawing motion, make a pocket. Season the oysters with salt and pepper; sauté in 1 tablespoon butter and some of the oyster liquid only until the edges begin to curl; drain. Stuff each steak with three oysters, wrap with a slice of bacon and secure with a toothpick. Broil or sauté. Heat the remaining butter until light brown, add the parsley or chives, and pour over the cooked steaks. Serves 4.

THE WILLIAMSBURG INN
Williamsburg

WILLIAMSBURG INN

This genteel inn, modeled from the English Regency period, was built initially for scholars who came to study the restoration of Williamsburg. In past years, the inn has become better known as a sort of "decompression chamber." Only a helicopter ride away from Washington, it is now the official resting place for visiting foreign dignitaries suffering from jet lag.

As you enter this insular oasis via the circular drive, you are greeted by a doorman whose warm service adds to the regal feeling you get in the presence of tasteful grandeur. Maybe it's the Regency décor's oriental influence that renders a subtle tranquility. You inwardly murmur, "Oh yes, I could get used to this." Then, you come upon a family portrait, complete with servants, from the eighteenth century. Today, the painting you see has been restored to the original, but when it was found some years ago, the original black faces of the servants had been painted over with white. Apparently, the inheritors of the painting tried to repaint history to reflect the needs of their time. The restorers have unmasked the cover-up, and today the painting hangs above the stairway near the entrance to the Regency Dining Room.

As I walked into the dining room I could understand why the VIP's of the world dine here. A sea of silver, gleaming beneath candlelight, sets the mood for a relaxing evening. Cocktails, with an appetizer of Smoked Salmon, tweaked my taste buds for the succulent Rack of Lamb, which I enjoyed with a light dry wine. My dinner companion chose a lower-calorie Poached Salmon that offered a lovely presentation. Then, while enjoying this classic American cuisine with continental overtones, the room was engulfed with music. An orchestra dramatically ascended into the room from the floor below. Had I not been so surprised, I would have applauded. Before dessert, which I will verbally applaud, my dinner companion introduced me to Stilton cheese—a delicious discovery.

I sampled four desserts, which included the Pecan Bar,

Black Forest Cake, Rum Cream Pie and a Sacher-Torte. To choose the best is like deciding which of your children you love the most.

I could easily spend a week at this five-star hotel, and most of that time would be spent in the Regency Room.

The Williamsburg Inn is located on Francis Street. Meals are served daily. Breakfast is from 7:30 a.m. until 10:00 a.m.; lunch is from noon until 2:00 p.m.; and dinner is from 6:30 p.m. until 9:30 p.m. For reservations (required for dinner) call (804) 229-1000.

THE WILLIAMSBURG INN'S PECAN BARS

¾ cup butter
¾ cup sugar
2 eggs
rind of one lemon, grated

3 cups sifted all-purpose flour
½ teaspoon baking powder

Cream the butter and sugar; add the eggs and lemon rind and beat well. Sift the flour and baking powder together; add to the creamed mixture and beat well. Chill the dough until it is firm enough to handle. Preheat the oven to 375 degrees. Press the dough onto the bottom of two greased and floured 9-inch by 9-inch by 2-inch pans and prick all over with a fork. Bake 12 to 15 minutes or until the dough looks half done. Remove from the oven and set aside.

Pecan Topping:
1 cup butter
1 cup light brown sugar, packed

1 cup honey
¼ cup whipping cream
3 cups pecans, chopped

Reduce oven to 350 degrees. Put the butter, sugar and honey in a deep, heavy saucepan; boil, stirring for 5 minutes. Remove from heat. Cool slightly and add the cream and chopped pecans; mix well. Spread the topping evenly over the surface of the partially baked dough with a greased wooden spoon. Bake for 30 to 35 minutes. Cool and cut into 1-inch by 2-inch bars. Yields 54 bars.

THE WILLIAMSBURG INN'S FANTASIO OMELET

1 medium apple
1 slice stale bread
¼ cup butter, divided
2 ounces sausage
1 teaspoon chopped walnuts
 or pecans

3 eggs
1 tablespoon light cream
salt and pepper to taste
¼ cup Cheddar cheese,
 shredded

Peel and dice the apple. Trim the bread and cut into croutons. Fry the croutons until brown and crisp in 1 tablespoon of butter, turning to brown all sides; reserve. Crumble the sausage and sauté until cooked through; drain and reserve. Sauté the apple in the sausage drippings and, when it is almost done, add the chopped nuts. Combine the croutons, sausage, apple and nuts; set aside. Beat the eggs and cream together until the mixture is light and foamy. Add salt and pepper to taste. Heat the remaining butter in an omelet pan over high heat; remove the pan from heat. Add the eggs and return to heat. When the eggs begin to set, lift the edges with a fork or spatula so that any uncooked egg will run to the bottom of the pan. Shake the pan occasionally to prevent sticking. When eggs are set, mound the apple mixture and the cheese on half of the omelet; fold it, and roll it onto a plate. Serves 2 to 3.

THE IRON GATE HOUSE
Virginia Beach

THE IRON GATE HOUSE

There are those among us who harbor such an aversion to certain school subjects that we will go to extraordinary lengths to avoid contact, even after graduation. I easily identified with the woman who refused to sit in the main dining room at The Iron Gate House, formerly a private girls' school, because math was taught there in front of the fireplace. She was, though, more than happy to be seated on the porch where the subject of theology, which she had thoroughly enjoyed, was taught.

It's funny how we are so amenable to suggestion, because after learning that story, Daintry and I suddenly found the front porch extremely enticing. Silly? Probably, but when dining out, it is my philosophy that one should enjoy the atmosphere as much as the food.

The Iron Gate's philosophy is: "We taste with our eyes as well as our tongues." Hence, their food is not only appetizing but also well presented. With a decided leaning toward French cuisine, their Camembert Frit appetizer makes both an attractive and succulent way to begin your meal. This first course was accompanied with the house white wine, which is subtle and dry with faint fruit overtones. The green salad that followed was typically French in simplicity and served with a piquant dressing. This balanced well with our dessert of Brandy Alexander Cheesecake, which was ostentatiously rich and wonderful.

If you wish to indulge in lighter fare, The Iron Gate has two fixed-price menus. For guests who call in advance, they are happy to prepare a vegetarian dish or a low-calorie seafood entrée, both served with salad.

I didn't ask what courses had been taught in their Parisian Cellar Dining Room because next time I intend to dine in that intimate atmosphere, unhindered by any schoolroom prejudices.

The Iron Gate is located at the corner of 36th Street and Atlantic Avenue in Virginia Beach. Dinner is served Tuesday

190

through Thursday from 5:30 p.m. until 10:00 p.m., on Friday from 5:30 p.m. until 11:00 p.m., and on Saturday from 6:00 p.m. until 11:00 p.m. For reservations (recommended) call (804) 422-5748.

THE IRON GATE'S CAMEMBERT FRIT

1 5-ounce tin of Camembert
1 cup flour
¼ cup cornstarch
1 to 2 teaspoons paprika
6 ounces beer
oil for deep frying
assorted fruit slices
2 ounces toasted almonds

Cut Camembert into quarters. Combine flour, cornstarch, paprika and beer, mixing until smooth. Dip Camembert into batter and gently ease into very hot oil and cook under 1 minute. Remove with slotted spoon as soon as cheese floats to top. Garnish with apple slices, banana slices, grapes, orange sections and toasted almonds. Serves 2.

THE IRON GATE'S OYSTERS CHESAPEAKE

½ pound bacon
1 medium onion, minced
2 medium green peppers, chopped
4 ounces chopped pimientos
3 to 4 dashes Tabasco sauce
2 tablespoons Worcestershire sauce
1 teaspoon oregano
1 lemon, juice only
dash of Old Bay Seasoning
4 ounces grated Gruyere cheese
16 oysters (Lynhaven or Bluepoint)
1 pound backfin crabmeat
rock salt

In a large skillet, semi-sauté bacon (not crisp) and set aside. Sauté onion and green peppers in bacon drippings until transparent. Chop bacon and return to skillet along with all ingredients except cheese, crabmeat and oysters. Set aside. Shuck oysters using blunt knife. Insert knife at hinge and twist until oyster opens. Sever tendon and remove oyster. Carefully remove any shells from crabmeat and fold meat into skillet, lowering heat and mixing thoroughly. Place 4 oysters each on 4 individual shells. Spoon crabmeat mixture evenly over oysters and sprinkle with cheese. Place on a bed of rock salt and bake at 400 degrees for 15 minutes until brown and bubbly. Serves 4.

THE IRON GATE'S BRANDY ALEXANDER CHEESECAKE

Graham Cracker Crust:

1¾ cups graham cracker crumbs

¾ cup melted butter
½ cup sugar

Mix all ingredients together and press into either an 8- or 9-inch springform pan.

Sour Cream Topping:

2 cups sour cream
1 teaspoon vanilla

⅓ cup sugar

Mix until well blended and set aside in refrigerator.

Cheesecake:

6 eggs
1 cup sugar
1 teaspoon vanilla
2¾ cups cream cheese
2 ounces brandy
3 ounces dark creme de cacao

dash of salt
dash of nutmeg (added to mixture)
sprinkle of nutmeg over top

In food processor or mixer combine eggs, sugar and vanilla and mix until well blended. Add cream cheese (cut in chunks) gradually until smoothly incorporated. Add brandy and creme de cacao and mix well. Add salt and nutmeg; mix thoroughly. Pour into springform pan and bake at 350 degrees for 1 hour to 1 hour and 15 minutes, turning pan halfway through baking. Remove from oven and shake gently to make sure it has congealed in the middle. Leave out for 5 minutes and top with Sour Cream Topping, spreading evenly for a smooth surface. Return to oven and bake 10 minutes more. Remove and place in refrigerator for at least 3 to 4 hours. Sprinkle nutmeg over top before serving. Yields 1 cake and serves 12.

MILTON WARREN'S
ICE HOUSE RESTAURANT
Virginia Beach

MILTON WARREN'S ICE HOUSE

The psychiatric field would argue about the influence a parent's career has on his or her offspring. But Milton Warren believes that growing up in a dietitian's home provided the impetus that launched him into the restaurant business. Warren's mother instilled the philosophy that makes his restaurant "a place to dine rather than just eat."

Built at the turn of the century, the ice house was insulated with ten- to twelve-inch cork walls and two feet of sawdust in the ceiling. The ingenuity of those early builders never ceases to amaze me. So many materials that current builders throw away were once put to very efficient uses.

Originally, the ice house was built to aid the local fishing industry, then expanded its operation to supply seasonal vacationers and local resort hotels.

The building was fast falling into disrepair when Warren salvaged this page of coastal history and converted the structure into a restaurant.

Sitting in the cozy dining room, Daintry and I were glad that he cared to create this intimate setting. The dining room is decorated with large ice hooks hung on weathered walls, and the tables are attractively set with linen cloths and fresh red roses.

We began by sampling two of their more popular appetizers, the Clam Oreganata and Oysters Rockefeller, and found both satisfied our seafood cravings.

I never think of ordering anything but seafood at the beach, and their Shrimp Scampi proved to be a light and luscious dieter's dream. Even with a nibble of their delicious homemade Popovers, there was still room for a sliver of their rich and creamy Cheesecake.

The restaurant also offers a small but adequate wine and beer selection with a strong emphasis on domestic vintages.

Milton Warren's Ice House is located at 604 Norfolk Avenue in Virginia Beach. Dinner is served daily from Memorial Day to Labor Day from 6:00 p.m. until 10:30 p.m., and Tuesday through Saturday during the winter months. For reservations (recommended) call (804) 422-2323.

ICE HOUSE'S CHEESECAKE

Topping:
1 pint sour cream   **2 teaspoons vanilla**
½ cup sugar

Place all ingredients in blender and mix until smooth. Refrigerate.

Pie Crust:
14-ounce package vanilla   **¼ cup butter**
  wafers   **1 teaspoon vanilla**
4 teaspoons sugar

Crush vanilla wafers in blender. Melt butter. In mixing bowl add wafers, sugar, melted butter and vanilla. Combine until well mixed. Press mixture into springform pan, covering bottom and sides. Set aside.

Filling:
3 8-ounce packages cream   **2 cups sugar**
  cheese   **2 teaspoons vanilla**
5 eggs

Soften cream cheese and place in electric blender with eggs, mixing until smooth. Add sugar, gradually, until well incorporated. Add vanilla, mixing to blend through. Pour into prepared crust and cook in a 325-degree oven for one and a half hours. Cool slightly, add topping and cook for another 15 minutes. Cool and place in refrigerator for 24 hours before serving. Yields 1 cake.

ICE HOUSE'S SEAFOOD NEPTUNE

4 tablespoons butter   **4 ounces crabmeat**
¼ cup white wine   **2 1-pound flounder fillets**
4 scallops   **2 tablespoons lemon juice**
4 shrimp, medium (cleaned)   **salt and pepper to taste**

In skillet, add butter and wine simultaneously. Sauté scallops, shrimp and crabmeat about 2 minutes. Slit each flounder along the side to form a pocket. Spoon sautéed mixture into cavities. Place on baking sheet or roasting pan. Pour remaining wine and butter sauce over top of fillets. Add lemon juice and salt and pepper to taste. Bake in 375-degree oven 10 to 15 minutes. Serves 4.

ICE HOUSE'S SCAMPI

4 teaspoons butter
2 ounces oil (olive or peanut)
2 to 3 garlic cloves, sliced
1 pound medium shrimp, shelled
½ teaspoon lemon juice

½ medium onion, chopped
1 tomato, chopped
½ of green pepper, chopped
1 teaspoon black pepper
1 teaspoon salt
1 tablespoon fresh parsley
¼ cup white wine

In skillet, melt butter, add oil and sauté garlic lightly. Add shrimp, cooking until it turns pink and begins to curl. Add lemon juice, onion, tomato, green pepper, black pepper, salt, parsley and wine. Cook only a minute or so until tender. Remove shrimp and pour sauce from skillet over top. Serves 4.

HILDA CROCKETT'S
CHESAPEAKE HOUSE
Tangier Island

HILDA CROCKETT'S CHESAPEAKE HOUSE

After the Captain Thomas ferry docked on Tangier Island, I pretended to wait for my daughter to come ashore. In actuality, I was eavesdropping on the island fishermen tying their nets. I wanted to hear their dialect, said to be an admixture of a Scotch brogue with Old English. The ferryboat captain told me that the self-conscious islanders won't speak to foreigners in that dialect—for outsiders, a totally different Southern dialect is spoken. I listened, and true to the captain's warning, I could not decipher one word.

The dialect, like the island, has an old world quality about it. Little appears to have changed from the early 1600s when Captain John Smith, on an exploratory mission for England, purchased Tangier for the price of two overcoats (a marginally better deal than the Indians got for Manhattan).

Since Tangier's roads are too narrow to permit cars, we walked a few blocks to the Chesapeake House for lunch. The restaurant is better known as Hilda Crockett's. The late Mrs. Crockett was a descendant of one of the early English families who settled the island.

Mrs. Crockett, with only a dime to her name, borrowed the money for the purchase of the white frame house. To make the payments, Mrs. Crockett concentrated on island ingenuity and began offering her delicious fare to hunters and "drummers," as salesmen were then called. Word of mouth spread Mrs. Crockett's fame and, as a consequence, today you have to wait in line for a meal, still made from her recipes.

The family-style meals are served on blue vinyl tablecloths, as fancy accessories would be as out of place in this low key atmosphere as gourmet cooking. We were served Crab Cakes, Clam Fritters, Ham, Potato Salad, Cole Slaw, Applesauce, Corn Custard, Homemade Bread and Pound Cake. There are no alcoholic beverages on the menu. My vote goes to the seafood and Corn Custard, while Daintry feels the Pound Cake deserves more than honorable mention.

After lunch, meandering over to the museum, I discovered that Tangier's first settler, William Crockett, had only a prayer book to read until 1775 when a merchant ship captain gave him a Bible. The islanders were so excited by this gift that nightly readings drew whole families.

Those Bible readings may have produced a long-reaching effect. Over two hundred years have passed, and there is still no alcoholism or need for a jail in this peaceful community. A little pamphlet explains, ". . . our quaint ways may be misunderstood as slow, but time is abundant here and we wish it not away."

Hilda Crockett's Chesapeake House is located on Main Street in Tangier Island. Access to Tangier is provided via the Reedville, Virginia, ferry (804/333-4656) or the Crisfield, Maryland, ferry (804/891-2240). Meals are served daily April 15 through October 15, from 7:00 a.m. until 6:00 p.m. For reservations (preferred for tour groups) call (804) 891-2331.

HILDA CROCKETT'S CRAB CAKES

2 slices bread
1 pound crabmeat
1 teaspoon Old Bay
  Seasoning
¼ teaspoon salt
1 tablespoon mayonnaise

1 tablespoon Worcestershire
  sauce
1 egg, beaten
1 teaspoon dry mustard
oil for frying

Break bread into crumbs and moisten with water. In a mixing bowl, combine all ingredients thoroughly. Shape into individual patty cakes and fry in oil until golden brown. Yields 10 to 12 cakes.

HILDA CROCKETT'S CLAM FRITTERS

2 cups clams
1 teaspoon pepper
1 cup pancake flour
½ teaspoon salt

1 beaten egg
milk (approximately ½ cup)
oil for frying

Put the clams through a meat grinder, add the pepper, and mix with pancake flour, salt, egg and enough milk to make a stiff batter. Drop by small spoonfuls into hot oil and fry until golden brown. Drain on paper towel. Serves 6.

HILDA CROCKETT'S CORN PUDDING

1 cup sugar (½ cup is sufficient)
3 tablespoons cornstarch
2 eggs, beaten
1 17-ounce can white cream-style corn

1 5⅓-ounce can evaporated milk
2 tablespoons butter

In a mixing bowl, combine sugar and cornstarch; add beaten eggs and mix until blended. Pour in the corn and milk and mix thoroughly. Grease a 1½-quart oven-proof casserole and pour in corn mixture. Dot with cubes of butter and bake in a 350-degree oven for approximately 1 hour. Serves 4 to 6.

HILDA CROCKETT'S POUND CAKE

3 sticks butter
3 cups sugar
6 eggs
2 tablespoons lemon extract

1 tablespoon vanilla extract
3 cups flour
1 teaspoon baking powder
1 cup milk

Prepare bundt cake pan by greasing with shortening and dusting with flour. Preheat oven to 350 degrees. In large bowl, cream butter and sugar until light and fluffy. Beat in eggs 2 at a time; continue beating while adding extracts. Sift flour and baking powder together. Reduce speed on mixer; add flour mixture alternately with milk, beginning and ending with flour. Bake for approximately 1 hour or until toothpick comes out clean. Do not overbake. Yields 1 cake.

INDEX

Apple Cobbler with Streusel Topping, Sky Chalet Country Inn 52
Baked Fruit, Buckhorn Inn 47
Boule de Neige, Hollymead Inn 67
Brownies, Chowning's Tavern 176
Chocolate Mousse, Miller's 83
Coeur à la Crème with Raspberry Sauce, Inn at Little Washington 108
Eyemouth Tart, Kenmore Inn 143
Grand Marnier Creme Torte, Bavarian Chef 95
Pecan Bars, Williamsburg Inn 187
Rich Cream Scones, Kenmore Inn 143

Pies:
Apple Pie, Warm Springs Inn 27
Buttermilk Pie, Gadsby's Tavern 132
Chocolate Pecan Pie, Virginian 87
French Silk Pie, Eagle 36
German Chocolate Pie, Wharf Deli & Pub 59
Irish Whiskey Pie, McCormick's Pub & Restaurant 55
Peanut Butter Pie, Buckhorn Inn 48
Pecan Pie, Ivy Inn 71
Praline Eggnog Pie, Wharf Deli & Pub 60
Rum Cream Pie, Christiana Campbell's Tavern 179

PIE CRUSTS
Apple Pie Crust, Warm Springs Inn 27
Graham Cracker Crust, Iron Gate House 192
Pastry Crust, King's Arms Tavern 184
Pastry Crust, Miller's 84
Vanilla Wafer Pie Crust, Milton Warren's Ice House 195

ENTREES
Fowl:
Cheddar Chicken, Edinburg Mill Restaurant 100
Chicken Barbara, Evans Farm Inn 127
Chicken in Tarragon Cream Sauce, Waterwheel Restaurant 24
Chicken Pot Pie, King's Arms Tavern 183
Chicken Salad, Wharf Deli & Pub 59
Chicken Virginia, Boar's Head Inn 64
Colonial Fried Chicken, Michie Tavern 80
Cornish Game Hen, Eagle 35
Curried Chicken, Laurel Brigade Inn 123
Roast Turkey "Marco Polo," Homestead 20
Roast Turkey with Peanut Dressing, Wayside Inn 104
Turkey Devonshire, Gadsby's Tavern 132

Meats:
Baked Sausage, La Petite Auberge 148

Broccoli Salad, Buckhorn Inn 47

Chicken Salad, Wharf Deli & Pub 59

Crabmeat with Hazelnuts, Sixty-Seven Waterloo 111

Cream of Watercress, Homestead 19

German Potato Salad, Hotel Roanoke 12

Pasta Light-Line Salad, Tobacco Company Restaurant 159

Salad and Dressing, Joseph Nichols Tavern 40

Sauerkraut Relish, Warm Springs Inn 28

Shrimp Salad, Hanover Tavern 167

Strawberry Salad, Portner's 139

SANDWICHES

Steak and Cheese Sandwich, Victorian Restaurant 31

Welsh Rarebit, Chowning's Tavern 175

SAUCES, STOCKS, GRAVIES AND DRESSINGS

Bearnaise Sauce, McCormick's Pub & Restaurant 56

Beurre Blanc, Sixty-Seven Waterloo 112

Blue Cheese Dressing, Fox Head Inn 156

Bordelaise Sauce, King's Court Tavern 120

Chocolate Kahlúa Sauce, Troutdale Dining Room 7

Demi-glace, Tobacco Company Restaurant 160

Dressing, Joseph Nicols Tavern 40

Feta, Basil, Shrimp & Tomato Sauce, Virginian 87

French Dressing, Half Way House 172

Hard Sauce, Laurel Brigade Inn 124

House Dressing, Sam Snead's Tavern 15

Mornay Sauce, Homestead 20

Peanut Dressing, Wayside Inn 104

Raisin Sauce, Boar's Head Inn 63

Raspberry Poppy Seed Dressing, Homestead 19

Red Eye Gravy, Martha Washington Inn 4

Rocket Fuel (barbecue sauce), Victorian Restaurant 31

Salsa Cilentro, Portner's 140

Sausage Gravy, Edinburg Mill Restaurant 99

Tomato Gravy, Edinburg Mill Restaurant 99

SOUPS

Caldo Gallego (bean soup), Virginian 88

Champagne Melon Soup, Ivy Inn 72

Cheese Cauliflower Soup, Sam Miller's Warehouse 164

Chicken Curry Broccoli Soup, Sam Snead's Tavern 15

Cream of Watercress, Homestead 19

Hungarian Goulash Soup, Bavarian Chef 96

Peanut Soup, Hotel Roanoke 11

Potato Soup, King's Court Tavern 119

Pumpkin Soup, Kings Landing 136

VEGETABLES AND FRUITS

Asparagus and Pea Casserole, Evans Farm Inn 128

Asparagus on Puff Pastry, Sixty-Seven Waterloo 112

Baked Carrots, Edinburg Mill Restaurant 100

Baked Fruit, Buckhorn Inn 47

Bourbon Sweet Potatoes, Olde Mudd Tavern 151

Carrots Cointreau, Hollymead Inn 68

Cheese Corn, Hanover Tavern 168

Corn Pudding, Hilda Crockett's Chesapeake House 200

Creamed Spinach, Olde Mudd Tavern 152

Cymling Cakes, Fox Head Inn 155

Frittata Zucchini, Prospect Hill 91

Green Beans, Half Way House 171

Marinated Carrots, Buckhorn Inn 48

Mexiskins, Sam Snead's Tavern 16

Stewed Apples, Hanover Tavern 167

Stewed Tomatoes, Michie Tavern 79

Stuffed Cabbage Rolls, Joseph Nichols Tavern 39

Zucchini in Tomato Sauce, Olde Mudd Tavern 151

Library of Congress Cataloging in Publication Data

O'Brien, Dawn.
  Virginia's historic restaurants and their recipes.

  Includes index.
  1. Cookery, American—Virginia.   2. Restaurants,
lunch rooms, etc.—Virginia.   3. Historic buildings—
Virginia.   I. Title.
TX715.0'29   1984   641.5'09755   84-2801
ISBN 0-89587-037-1